Xhale to Xcel:

The Journey to My Healing

by

CHRISTEL WEST

Xhale to Xcel: The Journey to My Healing

Copyright © 2020 by Christel West

For inquiries please contact:
Contact the Author via website: www.ChristelWest.com.
Contact the Author via email: Christelwestyes@gmail.com
Contact the Publisher via email: ISpeakPublish@gmail.com

All Scriptures come from the New Living Translation (NLT), New American Standard Bible (NASB) and King James versions of the Holy Bible unless otherwise indicated.

Disclaimer

All the material contained in this book is provided for educational and informational purposes only. No responsibility can be taken for any results or outcomes resulting from the use of this material.

While every attempt has been made to provide information that is both accurate and effective, the author does not assume any responsibility for the accuracy or use/misuse of this information.

Printed in the United States of America

ISpeak Publishing Service
Little Rock, AR.
501-519-6996

ACKNOWLEDGMENTS

To my family: You loved me unconditionally through my confusion and uncertainty as I took the Journey to My Healing. I know it was challenging at times. Despite the challenges, you remained here for me. Thank you.

To my husband, Marco West: I am truly thankful for you having an ear to hear what God spoke to you concerning us … and having the courage to stand through all the mess for me to be able to deliver this message. You have loved me with a love that brings me peace and emotional fulfillment. Although you were challenged on all levels, your confession and your consistency in being here for me was unwavering. Thank you S.U.G.A., for being my anchor.

To Helaine R. Williams, Make It Plain Ministries: I have no doubt that our connection is Divine. You never questioned the revelations I have had along my journey. You have always "gotten me"! I don't have many people about whom I can say that. Helaine, your ability to take my complexity, break it down and help me deliver my stories the way you do is truly a gift from God. You have served as my editor and my midwife to deliver not one, but two of my stories to the world … and I know we're not done. Thank you for your spirit of excellence and your ability to tap into the greatness within you to deliver heartfelt stories that transform lives. You are the G.O.A.T.!

To Tiffany Greene-Moorer, ISpeak Publishing: You have served as a mentor, leader, encourager and friend. I am so grateful for your publishing company and affiliates who have made this transition possible. Your expertise and willingness to serve allowed me to deliver both my stories through your company with ease. Your heart to empower, and not handicap, has positioned me to do it again and I am forever grateful to God for our Divine Connection. I am sure there will be more journeys to come that iSpeak publishing will help produce. Thank you for blazing the trail for new authors like myself.

To Christension Griffin, my spiritual ally: Thank you for assisting me in my healing journey, and especially for calling bull on things I wanted to excuse. You held me accountable and continued to speak life to the greatness that exists inside me. Your encouragement and understanding through this process helped me to stay the course. Thank you for telling me the truth about me. It's that truth that helped me see that I was living a lie ... and it was only the truth that would free me. Our friendship has been challenged several times. But, as the saying goes, "What's real can't be threatened." I have nothing to fear in our relationship. One thing I know for certain: The fact that we have endured, walked through and overcome so many things together is the foundation of a lifelong spiritual union.

To Carlos Tubbs, HTV Studios: Your gift. passion, tenacity and perseverance are rare. You have brought to life, with no reservations, every idea I have had. I am so thankful for your ability to expand every vision and bring it to life. I have watched you take nothing and make it something. In you I have the most amazing videographer/producer/creator ... one who assists me in executing projects with excellence. For that, Carlos, I can't thank you enough.

And thank You, God, for trusting me with the downloads and the understanding to transform my life and others. I am thankful that our relationship is finally happy, healthy and whole. What You have joined together, I will not allow anything or anybody to separate. I finally found the One I was looking for, and we have eternity to build and create together. God, I have You, and to have You is to have me. Together we are unstoppable, unlimited and infinite. I love You forever and always.

FOREWORDS

Xhale to Xcel: The Journey to My Healing is a phenomenal read. I was privileged to witness the discovery, the enlightenment and the revelations firsthand as author Christel West walked the path of her journey to heal herself and fulfill her God-given mandate as a healer, author and teacher. Her work focuses on self-empowerment, self-expression and healing the relationship with self.

I met Mrs. West in 2008 when she was exploring her passion as a mentor for young women in the meeting room of her detail shop. Even then, she was blessed with the gift of intuition, and she was willing to assist in healing others until there was breakthrough. I especially love and appreciate the fact that she was a catalyst in my own personal healing journey.

Per our discussion, Mrs. West's intentions and vision with writing *Xhale to Xcel: The Journey to My Healing* is to share the hurt and wisdom of her own journey to show that to "exhale" exploration and "inhale" inspiration puts you on the journey to "Xcel" in your own life. Now breathe as she takes you deeper into the stages of healing the self!

Dr. Christension Griffin

My mother's books — *The Journey Back to Me* and *Xhale to Xcel: The Journey to My Healing* — opened my eyes to the true opportunity I have in life. Through my mom's words, I was able to witness someone take control of their life and transform it into the life they desired. Watching my mom grow while writing these books has been a lesson in itself. Her tenacity in pushing through all the tests she's faced is inspiring. I have grown by watching her grow! I wouldn't be the woman I am today if she didn't face her fears and obstacles. Her genuine loving spirit allows you to be yourself, no matter the circumstances, and she truly cares. Her books are heartfelt and real! I am forever grateful to have her as my guide to living a fulfilling life.

Aleah Weaver

Table Of Contents

Bible versions used in this text:
King James Version (KJV)
New American Standard Bible (NASB)
New Living Translation (NLT)

INTRODUCTION

I'd never worked out prior to August 2018. When I started my workout journey that year, God began downloading spiritual revelations … snippets here and there.

Driven to make a record of these snippets, I wrote a little essay called "I Want a Divorce" — not a literal divorce from my spouse, but a mental divorce from my old self-image. It wasn't anybody's fault; it was just the place I was in my spirit as well as in my flesh. There were irreconcilable differences, and the two could no longer go on together. So, I had to divorce myself from the person my life experiences had shown me I was. I had to begin living a new life … the life God preordained for me.

Before I wrote the divorce letter, I didn't realize I was on life support. You think of "life support" as medical equipment, or some external force, that helps you to live. So, I was like, "OK. Well, I've attached myself to the job, I've attached myself to my relationships, I've attached myself to marriage, to all these things." When I realized this I said, "Wait a minute! If I don't ever stand in the truth of who I am, and if I'm on life support, that means people are holding onto the idea of who I used to be, which means they also continue to live from an external place. And they will never find the power within them."

It was almost like I had two friends in the room with me, discussing me — "Well, we need to just go on and pull the plug. We can't continue to watch her live like this." It was symbolic of friends who'd tell me that I had to stand in my truth, no matter what the cost might be.

It was I who pulled the plug. Afterward, I realized I could live without the things that had reduced me to life support — the unhealthy attachments we create, and without which we believe we can't exist because we never became fulfilled within ourselves. We thought we needed something, or somebody, outside of us to fulfill us.

When I pulled the plug, it wasn't just I who went through a grieving process. Even the people connected to me — people who were living the lie with me — went through that process. As it is in the natural, so it is in the spirit. They were grieving the person I used to be. They had problems embracing who I'd become because they, too, had attachments to that false reality ... that old me.

I pulled the plug, then the new me woke up. The first words I said were, "I want a divorce. I'm not going to get back on life support. Christel, you're going to have to learn how to breathe on your own, just like I had to learn how to breathe on my own. The reason you want me to go back to where I was before is because it's easier for us to breathe off somebody else than it is to breathe on our own" (codependency).

The flip side is that, again, when I started my workout journey, God began revealing things to me. *Wait a minute, Christel,* He said. *You have done relationships externally, but you need to be committed to an internal relationship with yourself. You've got to return to your first love. You have never loved yourself. You have loved and given everything to everybody else, but you have never given it to yourself. You committed to your job, for instance, because you needed the money for the family. But did you make a commitment to* you *so that* you *would be happy, healthy and whole ... emotionally, mentally, spiritually, socially and financially?*

I'd never done it, I realized. *I'd never done it.*

When you're on the treadmill, you're usually thinking of how long you're going to stay on there: *I'm going to do 30 minutes. I'm going to do 45 minutes.* And 20 minutes roll around and you're like, *I'm done. I'm tired.* Funny how we'll cheat on ourselves when we're on that treadmill, but we'll trip about somebody else cheating us ... or on us.

Matter of fact, all this time, you've been tripping about people doing things *to* you, but all the time they've been reflecting the disloyalty you've been showing yourself. You've been frustrated, because you've been expecting somebody to give you something you didn't have. You've got to sow it in order to reap it. You have not sown loyalty. You have not sown support. You have not sown faithfulness. You have not sown commitment. You have not given any of these things to yourself.

All this came to me while I was on that treadmill.

One day, I went to the gym in the afternoon instead of in the morning as usual. I was with my sister. Afterward, my sister said, "That was a really good, quick workout." The Spirit immediately hit me, and I said, "Yeah, quickies are good." In the natural, we use that term in reference to sex. Some men and women want a quick, sexual release. But in the world of exercise, quickies also exist. Sometimes you go to the gym and get a release through a short, but vigorous, workout. You're not looking for a man to lie with you and give you a sexual quickie, you're looking to give yourself a self-care quickie … the release you get from going on in there and getting what you need.

The other thing that hit me came when I was watching a video once. On it, they were talking about making love. The word that stood out to me was "make." Then I related it to baking: How are you going to teach somebody to make love to you when you don't even know the ingredients — the things it will *take* for them to make love to you? The question came to me: *Do you even know how to make love to yourself? What things can you put together in order to have that intimacy with yourself?* This was not a reference to masturbation. This was about having true intimacy — a close familiarity of friendship, according to one online definition — with one's self.

But again, society teaches us to look outside ourselves. Even when we go to church, we are taught to look for things outside of us, and that has continued to perpetuate a cycle of unfulfillment. That's why we have broken marriages and other unfulfilled relationships. We're trying to give somebody something we don't have — completeness through self-knowledge and self-love.

Before my husband, Marco, showed up, I went from one relationship to the next. I didn't take time to find out who Christel was. There were certain things Marco would do that would remind me of my ex-husband. And I'd be like, *Oh no, here's this same old thing.* Well, I'd gone into a relationship with a different man — but nothing had changed in me. So, of course I was going to experience the same thing! When we encounter the same problems from relationship to relationship, we tend to blame the other person. And then we want to close ourselves off and declare that we don't trust anybody. *No, baby, the relationship you have with* yourself *is toxic. The problem is that you don't trust yourself.*

The ultimate question that came to me as I worked out was this: *OK, Christel, you made a commitment to your husband. Do you trust that you're going to keep this commitment? Do you even know what a commitment is, or what that looks like? If you don't trust* you, *how can you expect to ever trust anybody else?*

Sometime later, I was reading my Bible and came upon Revelation 2:4, where Jesus, in the letter to the church at Ephesus, said, "But I have this against you, that you have left your first love" (NASB) and urged a return to that love. The Scripture hit me like a ton of bricks. "God, that is so good to me," I said. It was good in terms of helping me understand the reason I had a string of failed personal and business relationships behind me. I was not in touch with the person who should have represented my first earthly love — me — and, therefore, I was not healthy. And I realized that I had so much emotional toxicity inside of me that I was starving.

It's not enough for you to pine for the healthy relationship that has eluded you. You've got to get to the root of why you reject commitment to *you*, yet you'll commit to somebody else and say that it's love. Getting to the root of your problem lays the foundation for healing marriages and developing other healthy relationships.

CHAPTER ONE

Life Support

Try not to confuse attachment with love. Attachment is about fear and dependency and has more to do with love of self than love of another. Love without attachment is the purest love because it isn't about what others can give you because you're empty. It is about what you can give others because you're already full.

Yasmine Mogahed

Two women stand over a third, wringing their hands and discussing her condition as she lies motionless in a hospital bed.

Oh, poor Christel. I can't believe the only things keeping her alive are the things she's told herself that she needs to survive. I can't believe that the only things she thinks she's worthy of are disappointment, hurt, pain and unhealthy sacrifice. I can't believe she's convinced that her life is about everyone else and not her. Looking at her plugged into these lies — watching her just exist, rather than live — is so painful. I believe her spirit is ready to be free. I think it's time to pull the plug.

Nooooo! She's not breathing on her own. These lies are what's keeping her alive.

I don't want her to live like this anymore. It's selfish to keep her like this. We must pull the plug.

If we must, why don't we first remind Christel of who she is? She can hear us.

Do you really believe that will work?

It might. She's in a coma, but they did say she can hear us. Let's remind her of who she is.

The unfortunate truth is that, in most relationships, the only thing that's provided for is the physical/flesh. The *spirit* of Christel had never received words that would give her life. So, while her flesh lies in a coma, the friends begin to speak to her spirit.

Christel, you are a woman of wisdom ... powerful, unique, resilient, a beautiful soul. Your destiny awaits you. It's time for you to wake up and get up. We can no longer watch you live plugged into these lies, so we've got to pull the plug. You will never know who or what you could be if you stay on life support. It's time for your heart to pump love and not lies, so the decision has been made — life.

Doctor, pull the plug.

The plug is pulled. The patient flatlines because she doesn't know how to live independently of the lies that had become part of her existence.

Autopsy Report 1

Name: Christel West

Cause of death: Heart disease (inherited from Christel's father, and the cause of his death); heartbreak (Christel's heart was broken); heart attacks (the heart represents one's subconscious programming. Christel was defensive and easily offended by others, so her heart felt attacked); heart murmur (Christel's heart had holes in it after being attacked — therefore, it couldn't hold love); heart failure (Christel's heart was failing due to lack of love, lack of connection, lack of flow).

Autopsy Report 2

Name: Christel West

Identified by: Mother's DNA (rejection and emotional detachment)

Cause of death: Addiction to rejection/abandonment
Symptoms:
1. Anger
2. Bitterness
3. Resentfulness
4. Guilt
5. Shame
6. Emptiness
7. Fear
8. Insecurity
9. Depression
10. Isolation
11. Lack of connection

Conclusion: Christel wanted to be loved and accepted. The lack of healthy connections caused her death.

CHAPTER TWO

WHAT BIT ME?

I nterestingly, the same poison that's in a snake bite is used to heal the person it bites. Many times, people run from the thing that hurts them, but it's that very thing that's going to heal them. But they've got to first identify what bit them in order to create the serum that's going to heal them.

So ... what bit me?

When we're in pain, the doctor asks us, "How bad does it hurt?" We are our own physicians; reference to the proverb "Physician, heal yourself!" appears in Luke 4:23. But we don't ever ask ourselves, "Why do I feel like this?" How can life present us with what we need to create the serum to heal if we never identify what's hurting us? Do we want to treat the symptoms only?

I can see now how so much of our lives in the physical realm is tied to the spiritual realm. If you're not spiritually aware, you'll think it's normal. But it's not. What you're experiencing in the physical realm is also what you're experiencing in the spiritual realm, but you don't take the time to identify that. You just keep moving past it.

Somebody once asked me, "Why is it that when our back gets up against the wall, *then* we pray? Why don't we pray all the time?"

"It's because we get comfortable," I replied. "We get complacent. Then, when we're threatened and our back gets up against the wall, we tap into the power within us. Why? We know that if something doesn't happen, we're sunk."

Now when our back gets up against the wall, our frequency changes. We aren't praying namby-pamby prayers anymore; we're praying with authority. When our frequency changes, God picks up on that frequency and He delivers — *Oh, she's serious. She has tapped into the Queen inside her. She is a creator, declaring what shall be.* Then what? Whoosh! Right there. But it's not until our back gets up against the wall that we really tap into the power within us. In our times of trouble, God is trying to show us how powerful we are: *See? It's been in you all the time,* He'll tell us.

As Ephesians 3:20 says, He is "is able to do exceeding abundantly above all that we ask or think, according to *the power that worketh in us*" (KJV). We must plug into the original source. Where is your power coming from? Are you even plugged into the original source? And what condition is your power conduction device in? When you need a charger for your phone, you may not charge it most effectively if you get a secondhand, or off-brand, cord. The current isn't strong enough to give you what you need to power up. How many times have we tried to plug into a source and the current wasn't strong enough to give us what we need? You've got to know *where* to plug — as well as have the proper equipment — to be powered up to do what it takes to make the connection. But what do we do? Settle: "Oh, I've got 10 percent. I can go on with that." No, you need 100 percent!

When we start to pay attention, we'll find that God is speaking through everything. Because we're not aware of it, we just think, "Oh my phone isn't charging." No. God is warning us: *You are not connected.*

It's not by chance that we go through anything we go through. Life is nothing but a series of tests and lessons. If we don't pass a test, we get to take it again. When we pass, it's a lesson. The lesson isn't for us; it's for somebody else. But we get in our feelings, and we miss the point.

Here's a quote I use: "As long as I was in the picture, I couldn't see the frame." When I got in that gym, I realized that I was the problem. As long as I was in the picture, it was everybody else's fault. Our story doesn't change until we get out of the picture.

I live in Greenbrier and, until the end of January 2020, I ran an adult day care center in southwest Little Rock. The two cities are about 41 miles apart, and the gym at which I worked out was near the center. I'd get up at 4:30 a.m., be out of the house by 5, and make it to the gym by 6. This was how serious I was about creating a healthy, committed relationships with myself. When I got completely down and wanted to be delivered, it didn't matter what time I got up. I wanted what God had for me. The question was, how bad did I want it? My answer was, I wanted it so bad that I was willing to get up extra-early for it.

That's love. But people confuse self-care with self-love. "I'm supposed to get my nails and my hair done," they say. That's self-care. Self-love is you giving to yourself. Giving your soul what it needs to be fulfilled.

But you have done what so many others have done — looked outside yourself for fulfillment, when it's been in you all along. Jesus said to "seek, and ye shall find" (Matthew 7:7). He didn't tell you to look out there. Look within.

Consider Eve and her story in the book of Genesis in the Bible. Eve had everything. God *gave* her everything. But she threw it all away when she listened to a voice outside of herself … a voice who convinced her that God was with-holding something from her and that she was, therefore, missing out. What do we do? Start listening to voices out-side of ourselves. That's when the separation between our head and our heart begins — when we start listening to the external voices instead of the internal ones. We've got everything we need pertaining to life and godliness (2 Peter 1:3). When Eve listened to that outside voice — the voice of the serpent — that's when the duality, the separation, came. Then what happened? She and Adam were kicked out of the Garden of Eden. It wasn't about being *physically* kicked out of the garden; it was about *spiritual* eviction … losing that close relationship with God and, therefore, becoming mentally compromised.

Eve's story reflects our unfortunate decision to listen to other people and what they say about us. Doing so causes chaos and turmoil for us. In order for us to get back to the garden, where all things are provided, we must get our head and our heart in alignment with who *God* said we are; not what *man* says we are. To get back to the garden, we've got to come back to the truth. Who we are is enough. No situation or circumstance can take us out. Nobody can take anything from us. Our value doesn't go down because someone else fails to see it. But we allow the other per-son's short-sightedness to diminish how we see ourselves. It's not what other people say about us; it's what we say about ourselves! When we start talking to ourselves about ourselves, and we accept the truth of who and what God says we are, then things change.

Are you brooding or complaining about how badly somebody treated you? The person you believe wronged you wasn't the cause of your pain and unhappiness. That person simply brought out the pain and unhappiness that was already in you. In my case, I'd exhibited addiction behaviors in my past relationships. When my addiction was no longer fed in a relationship, I would go through withdrawals. It was in this moment that I could (a) live in the present and feel the pain, bringing it into consciousness to transmute the negative energy and create what I truly desired, or (b) go on to a different relationship and take the same hit.

The first step to overcoming an addiction is to admit that you are an addict. When threatened with the possibility of being alone, I would look for ways to self-medicate so that I wouldn't have to feel. The feelings wanted to be accepted. But, because I attached my identity to the feeling, I ran from it. I believed the feelings were who I was, so instead of accepting them I resisted them, causing myself more suffering. When you face your truth, you find your power. As long as I ran from the truth, I gave my power away. When I accepted the truth, I took my power back. The root cause of this addiction was my never having had a connection with my parents. My soul longed for connection. I identified only with the fear of not being connected in my relationships. Although I desired connection, I never had the exposure, so I ran from what I wanted and feared what I never had. Crazy, right?

CHAPTER THREE

I Want A Divorce

I, Christel, flatlined because the disease in my heart got worse and worse. Nothing existed in my heart that could help me to keep living. In order for there to be a rebirth, and for me to become resurrected from the dead, I had to have a heart transplant. The old heart needed to be replaced by a heart that chose love above anything else ... the heart of God, a heart by which I would love myself and others unconditionally. I had to leave behind the world I once knew and cross over into eternity, where all things are unlimited, and I can therefore have whatever I like.

My life without limits begins NOW.

The plug had been pulled. She had flatlined. But, amazingly, her heart starts to beat again. Her eyes open. She begins to see the truth. Slowly, she sits up and looks around. She opens her mouth, and says ...

I want a divorce.

I want a divorce on the grounds of irreconcilable differences. "Irreconcilable differences" is grounds for a no-fault divorce, which means neither party committed any inculpatory act such as adultery, abandonment or extreme cruelty. In other words, no-fault divorce is just like it sounds — no single party is at fault for the breakdown of the marriage.

I have been married to the brokenness, hurt, disappointment, pain, loneliness, discouragement, fear, unforgiveness, doubt, low self-esteem ... and the lack of intimacy, communication, attention or quality time. One minute, things are good; the next minute, things shift and there's an expectation of me to be somebody I'm not, instead of acceptance of me as I am. I'm too big. I'm not experienced enough. I'm boring in bed. I'm seeking attention elsewhere ... cheating, wearing the title of spouse but not embodying that title. I'm broke, never satisfied, uncommitted, undisciplined, selfish, self-centered.

So, I want a divorce. I no longer want to be married to someone who refuses to honor me, cherish me, support me and love me through the good and bad. I no longer want to be married to someone who uses words to discourage and condemn me, rather than teaching me the things of which I lack under-standing. I no longer want to be married to someone who isn't willing to love me unconditionally, who doesn't make me a priority, who is always focused on themselves. I no longer want to be in a marriage where I can't use my voice and am never listened to; a marriage in which I'm always having to defend myself. I can't go on like this. This marriage is unhealthy, and it has destroyed my self-esteem, self-confidence and self-love.

I have lost myself in you, but the time has come that I must let go. I must cut the cord — end the unhealthy attachment I have created through this union. If I don't, I am going to lose my life; the only thing that will remain is my existence. I love you, but I love me more. As much as it hurts, we can no longer walk together as one. This is where I draw a line in the sand and say goodbye to you, the one with whom I have spent the majority of my life. You taught me much. Our union was nec-essary because I needed you at the time. You helped me grow into the woman I am today. I appreciate you for trying to hold onto the idea of love, but one of us had to be stronger and make the decision for us to part company so that we both can be free.

I forgive you and hold no hard feelings toward you. I also forgive me for staying so long. You could only do what I allowed. You're not happy with me any longer because I've grown, and we don't see eye to eye anymore. I'm not happy with you because you're choosing to stay the same. So, let's give each other what we need to go and grow. I know this is the best decision for us both. I love you and I thank you for being a part of my journey, but it's time for me to move on. I must see what else life has for me ... and I can't, as long as I hold on to you. I release you; you are free to go.

This divorce letter is one I have written to myself. The truth of who I am no longer needs nor desires to be married to the lie of who I was. It was a must for me to divorce that story. I was in covenant with all my pain, hurt, shame, guilt, unforgiveness, and the list goes on. My life experiences caused me to believe that this was who I was and all I would ever be. I divorced those lies so that I could marry the truth.

CHAPTER FOUR

STDs: Problems
vs. Solutions

I was on life support, due to having an STD.

STDs are a topic that needs to be discussed. But nobody's talking about it, because some people may not know they're infected. I didn't know I was infected. But now that I have found out the truth, I will share it. We all know what an STD is, right? We know what the doctor says it is: a sexually transmitted disease. Well, I didn't have a *sexually* transmitted disease. I had a *spiritually* transmitted disease.

Some of you don't know that you have a spiritually transmitted disease. How did you get it? You allowed other people to penetrate your subconscious with their beliefs, their thoughts, their ideas and their perceptions ... and you've been walking around infected.

I was certainly walking around infected, and I didn't know it. In the natural, we know to protect ourselves from disease. We know we have to put on protection before we become sexually intimate with another. But look at all the people we have allowed to be intimate with us spiritually! We have received seed from them while failing to use protection. And everything starts off as seed, right?

The things people say to us are seeds. We sometimes take that seed, nurture it and produce what has been said. This is how generational curses are handed down. I received and nurtured bad seed and didn't realize that I was spiritually infected. That's why, when the right word came along, I was unable to receive it. I was unable to be fruitful, to multiply, to see the abundance I wanted in my life. My spiritually transmitted disease was handed down to me through DNA — through my receipt of seed from people imparting *their* truth.

Excuse me, but I'm just going to break it down using a little sexual biology. The consciousness is like a male's penis; the subconscious is like a female's vagina. It takes conscious thought to penetrate the subconscious in order to plant seed. What I was doing unknowingly was receiving seed from people who didn't know who *they* were, and certainly couldn't tell *me* who *I* was. Yet, I received what they said and reproduced it, which led to my having an identity crisis. I became what everybody else told me I should be, never giving birth to the truth of who God created me to be.

Jesus, in His Parable of the Sower, refers to the sower who sowed seeds in four different locations, three of them unfruitful ... by the wayside (the seeds couldn't penetrate the ground, therefore, birds ate them), stony ground (which resulted in plants that wilted and died because they didn't develop deep enough roots) and thorny ground (which resulted in the seeds being overcome by them). Well, I was infected ground ... infected by bad seeds. What I kept receiving was *familiar* word, but not the word of truth. Therefore, I kept reproducing the things I did not want. In the book of Genesis, Adam and Eve are told to be fruitful and multiply. How can I be fruitful and multiply if I'm infected with a spiritually transmitted disease ... one that resulted from my receipt of word-seed from people who were also infected?

My STD affected my romantic relationships, too. A hard truth I had to accept was that I'd wanted someone to love me for me, despite not even knowing who "me" was. I wanted someone to love the *idea* of me. I actually fell in love with the idea of love, and never knew what real love looked or felt like. I never knew the real me.

Everything you have experienced is an illusion according to the flesh, but it's designed to give you a spiritual understanding of what you're actually walking through. When God created you, He created you whole. He created you as one. You didn't understand oneness in the flesh. So, your spiritual journey involves coming back into unity with yourself, moving into a place where the conscious and subconscious align. There, you can be fruitful and multiply.

In the natural, we lay down with a man and we get pregnant. We're told, "You don't have sex before marriage; you don't reproduce before marriage." The Holy Spirit, meanwhile, is conveying this: *Don't go and make children with the wrong thinking that's been handed down to you.* When we take consciousness and subconsciousness and marry them, we have oneness. The head and the heart are in alignment; now we can manifest what we desire. But because we've been infected with an STD, we have not been able to produce anything.

As I've stated, we can catch an STD from the word-seeds of those whose lives don't reflect the results we want to see in our lives. So how do we heal ourselves? By receiving seed from people whose lives *do* reflect the results we want to see, and who speak our desired results into our lives. In order to heal my spiritually transmitted disease, I had to find people who had my results, who had my antibiotics, who had actually taken the journey to get free from the thing what had once infected them. If you are tired of not getting the results you say you desire for your life, check to see if you've got an STD. It could be that you are reproducing an undesirable seed somebody else planted in you.

We have to become our own case study. That's how I identified my spiritually transmitted disease. I began looking at my life to see where I was falling short. I realized I was receiving seed from people who did not have my results. Therefore, when the Spirit spoke to me, I couldn't trust what I was hearing! I had trust issues.

Once I realized I had this STD, I began connecting with people who had my results. I started listening to what *they* were saying. *Their* consciousness, *their* understanding, penetrated *my* subconscious. I began to receive a different type of seed, which meant I could give birth to something different. I was no longer sitting at the feet of people who caused my infection and were unable to heal it. I was tapped into those who were able to help me heal.

A major symptom of a spiritually transmitted disease is the absence in your life of the fruit of what God said is yours. Specifically, the way to identify whether you're infected is to look at the symptoms. Are you struggling in your finances, your health, your relationships? You probably got your STD when you received something that did not align with what and who God says you are, and as a result, "many are weak and sickly among you, and many sleep" (1 Cor. 11:30, KJV). Maybe it's yourself you've listened to and gotten the wrong information from. And you've listened to yourself for so long, without receiving proper counsel, that you are stuck in your STD. Your land — rather, your mind — has been barren. You have not been able to produce anything.

Often, it's the case that the bad seed you've taken in, and been infected by, was handed down by family members — in other words, you've become the continuation of a generational curse. The Scripture says to "be fruitful and multiply" (Genesis 9:7), but you've been multiplying the things you don't want … things that have been replicated in your bloodline from generation to generation. How are you going to be fruitful and multiply if you're sitting in the presence of people who don't have your results? They can't penetrate your subconscious to plant a good seed for you to nurture that seed and give birth. If you don't like what you're getting out of life, it's because nine times out of 10 you've reproduced and recycled what you're getting. Same old thoughts, same old behavior, same old results.

Again, I didn't realize that I had become infected by receiving seed from the wrong people. And nothing was going to change unless I changed how I saw myself. Because I didn't see myself properly, I fell prey to how other people saw me … people who had misidentified me. Their truth wasn't my truth, but I received their seed. As a result of it, I kept showing up with a mask on, pretending to be what everybody else wanted me to be.

So, I had to show up for me. I had to find me. I had to find the truth of me. I had to be honest with me … and, yes, I had to find someone who had my results. I no longer desired to be spiritually infected.

You can give birth to what you really want in your life. You are the creator of your reality. To change that reality for the better, I would advise you to be careful of whom you listen to. Don't let just anybody plant word-seeds in you! Matter of fact, don't let just anybody plant eye-seeds in you, either! Seed gets to you through your bodily gates … your eye gates as well as your ear gates. Make sure you are watching, and listening to, people who have your results. Those are the people you want to impregnate you. Those are the people you want to plant seed in your subconscious, because your subconscious is where your power is. You have to be sure that you're nurturing the right things. So, give yourself permission to get the medication you need. Get yourself in the company of people who can help you heal so that you will not see the same thing that you saw in 2019, 2018 and earlier. Find a coach, find a mentor, find someone who is bearing the fruit you want to see in your life … somebody who has the antibiotics to clear up your particular STD (everyone has different issues). Find a church that teaches kingdom principles. Why? Because the kingdom is within us, and we need not look outside ourselves for what God gave us.

In the natural, we tell young people to "strap up" — in other words, use a condom during sex to avoid an untimely pregnancy. You need to strap up in the spirit realm. I can't emphasize enough that you've got to protect your thoughts. You've got to make sure you are wearing the helmet of salvation so that you won't receive bad seed and continue to produce things you don't want in your life. It's up to you. God gave you the power to save yourself. Nobody is coming to save you.

I went to hell. I went to the deep, dark parts of my soul to identify why nothing was happening *for* me, but everything was happening *to* me. I shifted my perception. Once I did, I realized that I'd become infected with an STD and was therefore unable to be fruitful, multiply, and replenish the earth with truth. I kept doing what everybody else was doing … giving the wrong seed to others. I can't emphasize enough that when we plant the wrong seed, we keep reproducing the same lies that negatively affect our quality of life.

In summary, *you* have got to be the change you want to see. Identify your STD. If you identify and confront the things you have chosen not to confront up to now, trace your symptoms back to the root. Determine why you keep seeing the same undesirable results over and over and over in your life. Then, seek to connect with people who have your results … the antibiotics to clear the infection that has existed within you and prevented you from being fruitful and multiplying. Once you do, you can be free, once and for all. It all starts with your thinking. Your subconscious will only reproduce the seeds that have been fed to it. It takes *conscious* thoughts to penetrate the subconscious and plant new seeds to bring forth a different harvest.

One day while I was at the gym, the Spirit said, *The reason you lacked commitment to the things I've told you to do is because subconsciously, you didn't believe you were worthy of all I said is rightfully yours.* I had to shift my thinking. Now, I don't let just anything, or anybody, penetrate my subconscious. I'm not going to let just anybody come and speak into my life, because I no longer desire to live with a spiritually transmitted disease.

Earlier I'd mentioned the act of "strapping up." Just as you do to avoid an unwanted pregnancy, you also strap up, or put on a condom, when you want to avoid a sexually transmitted disease. I say again that you need to strap up in the spirit realm, putting on the helmet of salvation lest the wrong person penetrate your subconscious mind with their truth and impregnate you with false doctrine. That's what you've been reproducing, and getting, generation after generation after generation. You've let the wrong person penetrate your subconscious and plant the wrong seeds. As a result, you've got a spiritually transmitted disease, and now your kids are spiritually infected. And then you want to beat them with the Bible, which you have failed to read or understand, and tell them to go to church. That is not going to work. You've got to clear up the infection in *you*, because you've been "tossed to and fro, and carried about with every wind of doctrine" (Ephesians 4:14). You've got to be rooted and grounded in love (Ephesians 3:17). But you have not been rooted and grounded. So, when somebody comes and says something — there you go! Look, if you're rooted and grounded in love, you won't move. Nobody can get you off your rocker!

Back to the farmer sowing the seed: Where is the seed landing? By the wayside? On stony ground? Among the thorns? On good ground?

In summary: All things start with a thought, and all words are seeds. So, who are you allowing to penetrate your subconscious with their seed? If you are suffering through spiritual miscarriages and spontaneous spiritual abortions, it's because you have received a seed God didn't plant. If you're not covering yourself, don't expect anybody else to cover you. It all starts with you. Be the change you want to see. Clear up that STD ... that spiritually transmitted disease.

CHAPTER FIVE

THE BREAKUP

*L*et me take you to the last weekend in 2019. I needed that weekend by myself.

Marco, my husband, and I had come together right after my 17-year previous marriage. We moved really, really fast. The entire time of this whirlwind courtship, I harbored uncertainty, wondering: *Should we, or shouldn't we?* We married, but the entire marriage had been a back-and-forth — unresolved dickering. As this particular weekend approached, the back-and-forth in full force, I told myself, *You've got to choose* you.

"Hey, listen. I don't think we should be together right now, because I don't feel the connect," I told Marco. "I just need to go and be by myself … I don't need to be with anybody."

That Friday, I got a bottle of wine and some candles, checked into a hotel in Little Rock and listened to my jazz music.

I'd also been led to go to the dollar store and buy some big sheets of poster paper. As I sat and enjoyed my wine, candles and jazz, I took each poster and wrote down in big letters these words … *Fear. Guilt. Anger. Shame. Hurt.* Around each word, I jotted down specific feelings and phrases associated with that word. I didn't know all this was in me.

I also wrote the word *Forgiveness.* This represented my forgiveness of myself, not anyone's forgiveness of me. Again. I had no idea I had all this in me.

I realized that my action really represented my pushing these negative emotions away from me, rather than drawing them to me. It's kind of like the pursuit of money — the less you pursue it, the more you draw it, but the more you pursue it, the farther you seem to push it away. Well, energy works the same way, especially in human relationships: I want you to experience my heart, so I'm doing all these things for you, trying to show you my heart. But all you can see is what I'm doing. You never experience my heart, because I'm trying to make you *see* my heart, rather than let you *feel* my heart. It's the difference between doing and being. Everything I would try to get people to see, they couldn't see. I was really pushing them away from me … which then caused me to feel rejected and abandoned.

Dissolve it in you, Christel, and it will dissolve around you, the Spirit said. My thought process had triggered all those suppressed feelings and emotions and, with the Spirit's prompting, allowed them to be understood and released. I knew that if I had not released them, I would continue to self-sabotage my relationships.

Saturday night, the second night of my weekend of solitude, I wrote more on my posters. Then the Holy Spirit said to go take a shower. I got in the shower. Now I am not one to sit down during a shower, but the Spirit said, *Sit down.* So, I sat. I let the water run over me and I began to thank God for the releasing of those emotions I had written down. This was like a baptism … I was washing all this old stuff off me and basking in the presence of God.

Then I heard the Spirit say, *Take your arms, wrap them around yourself and say, "I love you."* With my eyes closed, I took my arms and wrapped them around myself. Weeping, I said, "I love you." In that moment, I saw the little girl in me … but I saw her outside of me, spinning around happily. When I embraced myself, I freed her! God had given me a vision of this little girl, spinning freely around in front of me. And there I was in the shower, just bawling.

Then the Spirit said, *Now take your arms and wrap them around you again and tell the little girl in you, "Thank you for saving me."*

I was so done! God had shown me, through the process He'd walked me through, that there was nobody coming to save me ... I had to save myself. But I had to go through a process in order to save myself. The freeing of the little girl in me represented the process.

That was the end of December. We were crossing over into 2020. In 2019, I let the little girl in me go ... I freed her. But in 2020, I realized there were remnants of that little girl still working in me ... and I didn't know where these remnants were rooted.

I concluded that Marco and I might need to part company on a more permanent basis. "We can't do this," I told him.

"No. God told me you are my wife," he said.

"No, He didn't tell me that," I replied. "He told *you* that. No, this is something that I must do."

I adamantly told him that this time, I couldn't put anybody else before me. "I know you don't understand it," I said. "But when it comes to the things of God, sometimes we don't understand. It's not about comprehending; this is about obeying. I've got to go this way. There's no way around it." Now did I understand it? No. All I knew was that this was something I had to do.

Up to this point, I'd said yes to everybody else, and no to me. So now, here I was reversing this thing … saying no to Marco and yes to me. And he was frustrated. He was *mad*. He was upset.

"You made a commitment when you married me," he said.

"That's just a piece of paper," I replied. "A commitment is something that is a heart thing."

But he didn't get it. "No; you made a *commitment*! You're supposed to honor this *commitment* you made!"

"I hear that," I told him. "I understand that. But that isn't what I need to do. *This* is what I need to do."

In my first book, *The Journey Back to Me*, I asked: "Could it be that I parented myself the way my mother parented me?" My mother lives with Marco and me, so she was living with this back-and-forth we were going through. She was feeling the tug of it … that's her son-in-law; I'm her daughter. As was revealed in the first book, I'd had an issue with her choosing a man over me, Any time she would listen to him, I felt that she wasn't listening to me … and that would trigger me. So, I was triggered this particular day, when she witnessed our argument and saw Marco's point.

Then I stopped and said to myself, *Wait a minute. What is this I'm feeling?*

There's a feeling you have when you just don't want let things ride. It's kind of like, *I'm gonna wrestle with God until He blesses me.* That was my attitude — "I'm not letting You go, God, 'til this thing right here is off me."

Usually, when there's something in my gut that I need to release, I go and sit in the bathtub. I'll inhale what I want and exhale what I don't want. I went to the tub this particular day. There I was, inhaling and exhaling, inhaling and exhaling, and just weeping ... until the Holy Spirit said to me. *Christel, you're so afraid. You still carry rejection and abandonment from your mother.*

Yes! I was still carrying, and dealing with, those very burdens. My mother's failure to grasp my side of the disagreement with my husband triggered me. But it triggered me for the sake of my realization that it was no longer an issue of anybody rejecting me; it was an issue of me rejecting myself. Every time the Holy Spirit told me to do something, I would instead do what somebody else wanted me to do. The acceptance I was seeking from another, it was now time for me to give myself.

So, I said to the Spirit, "Oh, OK. I've got it!"

The Spirit wasn't finished, however.

The reason you've got to stand up for yourself, He added, *is because this is the end of your mother's life — you as she, that is — and where your life begins.*

"What are you saying, God?" I asked.

The reason you have to take a stand for yourself is because your mama chose a man over you. You weren't supposed to choose a man over you. You were supposed to choose you. *The way you save your soul, Christel, is to love and accept yourself.* That was the cycle-breaking stance I hadn't understood the need to take!

"I understand it now," I said.

I was able to go upstairs and talk to my mom. She had lacked understanding; I now had the wisdom to lead her, as well as myself, out of that lack. Then I went and shared with my daughter, who had repeated the family cycle of choosing a man over herself and/or her loved ones.

So that was the end of that. But the Spirit also dealt with me on the heart issue.

Physically, I'd had sexual partners, but I'd never had intimacy. I knew how to *physically* show up, but I didn't know how to *connect.* When I did a spiritual autopsy on myself, I realized I was a reproduction of my parents. They could only reproduce what they were. I saw why I had to die to what I was birthed into … rejection, abandonment and heart issues.

"OK, God," I said. "I think I get it." My daddy had heart disease, and he never talked about anything. And that was me, prior to taking the journey to my healing. I didn't talk about anything; I suppressed it. And I ended up with high blood pressure. All those different things went on in my daddy's body. All those self-inflicted feelings he never dealt with was proof that the devil didn't kill him …

the enemy within took him out. He'd never dealt with his emotions, his feelings; he'd never expressed them. Again, that was handed to me.

As it is in the natural, so it is in the spirit. You have a heart so that your body will function. But that's just your fleshly body. It functions without you even thinking about it. It does what it's supposed to do. If I was going to live the life Christ died to give us — life more abundant — then my spiritual heart had to open. It had to be awakened for me to experience this connection we all say we desire. I desired it, but I had not known how to access it. This is why I had to die and be born again of the Spirit.

As I'd stated earlier, we are a reproduction of our parents; they can only reproduce what they are. That means my life was a subconscious life, not a real one. It was a reflection of the programming handed down to me. In order for me to actually live, I had to walk out of that programming and walk into the truth of who God says I am and how I should function. In *The Journey Back to Me*, I discussed how my mother chose a man over me. My subconscious fear was that someone who claimed to love me would always choose somebody else over me and take their love away. The feelings of rejection and abandonment were running neck-and-neck with the heart issues.

I still had that desire to be Daddy's daughter. But we can love only according to the level of consciousness we're on. According to my daddy's level of consciousness, he gave me what he was able to give me. My idea that he was supposed to do "this, this, this and this" was an attachment I held onto. That attachment created an expectation. And that expectation created an idea that I was owed something. You can see why my husband never had a chance … my daddy didn't do what I needed him to do. Subconsciously, I was still looking for the provider and protector I'd never had. When I felt that my husband hadn't fulfilled those two roles, he became the enemy! Because I saw him, through my "pain body," as the enemy, I could never see him for who he really was. The same rejection I was feeling, I put on him — "You could have done something. You could have helped me pay these bills. I'm out here doing this and you're not doing that." I would be so frustrated, expecting him to play a role he didn't sign up for, and do what my daddy didn't do.

And here's the thing: He was trying to love me in a way I had never been loved. Because I didn't recognize that, I kept rejecting his love and looking for the love I never got. The love I wanted was always present, but I couldn't see it because I was in my pain body and had trust issues. I'd revert to the disappointed little girl whose daddy would tell her he was going to do something, but then fail to do it. My husband would try to give me instruction. But I rejected his word-seed, because of the light in which I saw him.

"I'm not going to listen to anything you say," I'd tell him. "Your word doesn't hold any weight, and I can't trust you." Whenever he tried to give me words to help me out of the bad mental place I was in, my response would be, "No, I don't want that; you keep that."

When I did something to hurt him, he would react in a way that made it appear that he was withdrawing all he'd given me. Then, he was *really* the enemy! He was doing the same thing my daddy did! So, my attitude was, "Now I'm coming for you. I'm going to try to hurt you like you hurt me."

Before he passed, my daddy and I had the opportunity to enjoy some time together. We would take fishing trips. I would cut his hair. We would drink beer and watch games. I had to accept what he had to give, because it was all I could get. It still left me without a real connection with him. So, when a man came into my life, I just accepted what I could get from him without having a real connection. I'd be all alone in the relationship, emotionally unfulfilled. And I'd blame the man when really, the blame was mine.

My fear concerning Marco was that if I allowed myself to be vulnerable and open my heart, I would choose him, but he would not choose me. Therefore, Marco had to accept what he could get, just as I had to accept what I could get in past relationships.

Bearing that biological soul tie of rejection and abandonment, I kept experiencing the same problems in all of my relationships because that's the energy I was vibrating from. I didn't realize that's what was going on; I just thought I was the victim. Now I'd mentioned earlier that life was a series of tests that we're destined to take again and again until we pass them. Similarly, conventional wisdom says you're going to repeat a cycle until you get it. Well, if you keep experiencing the same issues relationship after relationship, the problem is not the other person ... *you* are the common denominator! You feel rejection and abandonment because your relationship partners are under soul contract with you. Your spirit summons these partners to you because you are under contract to see those truths about yourself, truths to which you may have previously turned a blind eye. The relationship partner may change, but the contract is still in effect.

So, over the course of 40-something years, the issues of rejection and abandonment kept cycling back around and around and around in all my relationships. Things were never happening *for* me; they were happening *to* me. But I had a victim mentality. I was in my pain body. So, that's how I saw it ... "they" kept doing things to me.

If this is your reality, you need to get out of that story in order to see what's actually happening. Otherwise, you're going to keep seeing the same thing. That is why I kept drawing people who would be there for me for a while, then go away, then come back and be there for me for a while, then go away again. They were coming with a lesson. They were under soul contract — spiritual contract — with me to show me myself. They were there to try to free me from my attachments, which created expectation and led me to believe somebody owed me a debt.

When you feel someone owes you such a debt, how do you clear it? You clear it by making this declaration: *I have no attachments to you and no expectations of you based on what I think you should be. I accept you for who you are.* This allows love to flow through you. But when you have attachments to, and expectations of, another party, and that party fails to live up to those attachments and expectations, their perceived debt to you represents a blockage. You have to forgive people their debts to you so that *you* can be free.

In my case, I was stopping the flow of abundance *to* me because I wouldn't let abundance flow *out* of me. Again, Jesus said He came to give us life so that we could live life more abundantly. Abundance comes with an open heart, because love is what draws all good things to us. The reason those things are not being drawn to us is because we still function with this earthly heart. Our spiritual hearts haven't been awakened to allow us to experience the abundant life. So, we end up totally frustrated with God, asking

Him, "Why are you not doing [whatever]?" And God is asking us, *Why are* you *not doing it? Why won't you allow yourself to be vulnerable? Why won't you allow yourself to feel? What are you scared of?*

He asked me that. And I had to admit that I was scared of being hurt. I was scared of being made to feel ashamed. My fear was causing me to be limited in every area of my life. Thinking I had to be the strong one, I would intellectualize every doggone thing instead of letting myself feel it — because it hurt me to feel. Well, if we don't feel, we're not living! We're just existing ... going through the motions. It's not until we open our hearts up that we really live, that we really experience the bliss that life can be. But for the most part, we're just showing up.

While I ran from my feelings, Marco chased me. He had been chasing me the entire time we'd been together. He'd been in pursuit of me and I'd been running the other way, because subconsciously I feared he was going to do what everybody else did ... choose another.

But there he was, still chasing, still pursuing.

Granted, when he got angry or frustrated with me, he would tell me about myself. Now when you — out of your own pain and drama — hurt another, it also hurts to hear that you hurt them. When he told me what I did to him, I would get very *de*fensive as well as *off*ensive. I didn't want to hear those things about me. But I identified with them, rather than seeing them as just a behavior resulting from what had been handed down to me.

"Basically, you told me everything I'm not, or didn't do right," I said.

I had just wanted to be loved and accepted by my daddy. I just wanted Marco to love and accept me. Every time he told me what I was doing wrong, I was reduced to feeling like a lost little girl ... *Aw, Daddy doesn't love and accept me. I messed up again.* But when Marco *did* hear me, receive me, listen to or understand me. I felt I wasn't good enough for that treatment, and I ran from the feelings of rejection. That's why he had to chase me.

When *I* chose me, I had to learn to trust me. When I heard the Spirit say, *You've got to do this for you,* I had to trust that what I heard was what I heard. As a result of trusting myself, I not only saved my life; I was able to go about saving my children's lives.

Another thought about my following in the footsteps of my mother: I think a lot of women know what they should do, consciously. There's a Scripture, Romans 7:14-17, that says "So the trouble is not with the law, for it is spiritual and good. The trouble is with me, for I am all too human, a slave to sin. I don't really understand myself, for I want to do what is right, but I don't do it. Instead, I do what I hate. But if I know that what I am doing is wrong, this shows that I agree that the law is good. *So, I am not the one doing wrong; it is sin living in me that does it*" (NLT, emphasis mine). It's that DNA, those cells, those members working in you that cause you to be torn. It's no longer you; it's the spiritual warfare — your mama and daddy and ancestors who are causing you to be this way. That energy was all handed to you. What you're trying to do is break away from it ... cut the cord.

So, it's no longer me doing what I hate, it's the sin living in me. It's my internal war: Do I do with my mama did, or do I do what the Spirit is leading me to do? I had to cut the cord.

CHAPTER SIX

GRIEVING

G rieving is real. Letting go of emotional attachments is like losing the person who filled the void that existed within you. This experience leaves you feeling the same as you did before that person showed up, which forces you to get to the root of the release. Why was the root even created? It's what I've stated before. Fear, or lack, caused you to look outside yourself for what you already have. As a result, your existence and livelihood have been connected to that which is outside yourself.

Not only are you releasing the attachment, you're also releasing yourself to move forward in your life. When it's time to let go of what no longer serves you, the pain will be triggered. You must let that pain rise so you will get the healing you require. You must accept the fact that although you appeared awake, you were really asleep. Letting go is your wakeup call. It activates the suppressed pain/anger and serves as your alarm clock. When you press "snooze" on your alarm, you then will have to wait for the next alarm, and that may cause you to miss opportunities. Deciding to get up requires you to realize that it's time to accept things as they are ... a realization that leads to the root of your release. This moment serves as an awakening: What once was will be no more. You have consciously chosen to stop carrying the burden you have borne.

Let it go. Wake up and live.

Dr. Elisabeth Kubler-Ross, psychiatrist and author of the 1969 landmark *book On Death and Dying: What the Dying Have to Teach Doctors, Nurses, Clergy and Their Own Families,* outlined five stages of grief:

Denial: "This can't be happening to me."

Anger: "Why is this happening? Who is to blame?"

Bargaining: "Make this not happen, and in return I will ____."

Depression: "I'm too sad to do anything."

Acceptance: "I'm at peace with what is going to happen/has happened."

(A modified Kubler-Ross model adds two additional states: **Shock** — "Initial paralysis at hearing the bad news"

— before Denial, and **Testing** — "Seeking realistic solutions" — usually placed between Depression and Acceptance.)

To overcome my grief, I had to face, and answer, the question: *What healthy relationships have I seen in my life?* I had not seen a healthy relationship.

My former marriage was certainly not healthy. I knew I wasn't ready for that marriage, but I married anyway because of fear: fear of being alone, fear of what he would think or believe about me, fear of how others would look at me.

For nearly 20 years, I held onto that unhealthy relationship … holding onto potential. My ex was the unhealthy image I had of, and the unhealthy experience I had with, my daddy — the man I was still holding hostage to what I believed he should have done for me.

Let the dead bury their dead, the Holy Spirit said. *All that stuff is dead, Christel. Your father is dead. But you keep resurrecting him with your energy.*

And to think I didn't even know I had an attachment to my dead father. After all, we didn't have a relationship. It was the *lack* of the relationship that caused me to try to create one. I created it in honor of who I told myself he should have been. All this time, I still wanted Daddy to show up.

He's dead. Accept it and move on.

Now that I knew the truth, I could be free. I could intentionally release my dad.

This had to manifest externally for me to get it internally. God been showing me all along, but I was holding onto the attachment I'd created in my mind because of the void. That attachment had me blind.

And the word/spirit became flesh and Ralph, my ex-husband, arrived. Actually, he woke me up and freed me. I am grateful!! I couldn't see his spirit because I had him tied to a particular role, a particular image I had created mentally. We've all heard the phrase "mind over matter." Well, my mind created that false matter over and over and over again. But I thank God for a renewed mind and the ability to gather the pieces of my soul. I thank God for healing. For deliverance. For freedom. For independence. For oneness.

I remember a sermon I heard at church once. The theme was, "You Have to Stake Your Claim." I had to stake my claim. What was my claim? My life. Nobody can take it unless I lay it down. As the preacher had said, I'd been given the land to possess, but I'd given it away. Now that I'd slain Goliath (the false narrative I'd created and bought into), I could take it back ... repossess it.

This is why we have to evict all the crap with which we have filled our heads, hearts and souls. We have to get it out of us and disconnect from it, because such attachments create mental bills we must pay. The Word says to "owe no man any thing, but to love one another" (Romans 13:8a); it also instructs us that "with all thy getting get understanding" (Proverbs 4:7b, both KJV).

I have a clear title. There are no more liens holding me. "I'se free now!" I proclaim in my "Celie" voice (referring to the character in the book and movie *The Color Purple*). I'm loving it.

Our mothers, having bought into mental generational curses, unfortunately passed them on to us. They reflected, and passed along, codependency, neediness, fearfulness, loneliness, abandonment. They were little girls carrying motherhood roles. We, their children, were sent to save and lead them out, providing they were willing to accept responsibility for their part.

I release my idea that my mother should have been anything other than who she was. As long as I held her to that "other" title, I would never be able to experience the truth of who she was outside of my pain. She was still carrying all that weight of not being accepted. I would get aggravated because she would want to wear my perfume or get an outfit like mine. I would be like, "Mom, get your own identity," but the truth was that I had taken on *her* identity. At the same time, she had been trying to heal the little girl in her through me. But now that I have ascended, the separation of flesh can take place.

It seemed as though the roles had reversed, and they really had. I now know why the Spirit said for me to honor my mother and speak specific words to her at the Xhale to Xcel women's empowerment weekend event I hosted (more on that later). I'd been told that many her age would not face what she has faced and still walk alongside me; they would continue hiding. Her needy spirit, because I didn't understand it, would cause me to want to run and hide. I get it now. The little girl in me had not been freed and couldn't be until I released her from the soul tie I'd created. She wasn't strong enough to cut the cord. I had to, because this time I was birthing her out. The word became flesh, and she arrived.

To live peacefully simply means accepting things as they are. When we resist, we cause ourselves suffering. Acceptance is what keeps us in the present, in the now. When we resist, we remain unconscious. The process of changing first requires acceptance of what is. That allows us to bring what is unconscious to consciousness, which puts us in the position to transmute the energy we identify as negative.

The mind creates attachments based on the subconscious programming that exists in the brain. The mind receives the impulses/frequency from the brain and responds, creating experiences from the place of need, or lack. We already have everything we need, but we fail to live from that place because of the *illusion* of lack. Which, in turn, feeds the ego that has been created as a result of pain and suffering. The ego needs to be fed. It craves the false beliefs that have been created out of need. This is what causes us to identify with our mind instead of living in the present and *being*. Our mind creates matters. When we put our mind aside, so to speak, we are able to create solutions. We are able to place our mind over the matter, which puts us back in the position of power ... dissolving the illusions within and around us.

I am working on me daily. Letting go of my toxic thoughts and belief system internally and externally. I absolutely love who I'm becoming. She is the total package.

My life reflected what happened to me and would not allow me to see the truth of me. My vision was distorted; getting a clear picture required me to keep shifting. I had eyes to see but could not see. My eyesight limited me to the illusions I'd painted in my mind as a result of my life experiences. The truth was that these experiences (flesh consciousnesses) limited me to only what I could see. My soul work was not complete. I had to intentionally choose to continue digging daily to uncover the treasure that has been hidden in my earthen vessel.

The treasure is love. The treasure is me.

CHAPTER SEVEN

CONSCIOUSNESS, CONNECTION AND LOVE

*A*s I stated in Chapter Four, consciousness is like a penis; subconsciousness is like a vagina. It is our conscious thought that penetrates our subconscious mind, planting the seed for us to reproduce.

The Bible gives us Mary, the mother of Jesus, who became pregnant with Him despite having not been with a man. The reason Mary was able to receive the Holy Spirit and become pregnant with the Word that was spoken over her — the Word we know as Jesus — is because her conscious and subconscious were in alignment. How many times has God spoken a word over us that we were unable to receive, and which failed to take root, because of our spiritually transmitted disease?

Also, how many of us have mistakenly assumed that we are getting the aforementioned alignment via traditional sources … not realizing those sources, regardless of the high, trusted status they may hold, are failing us?

I'm going to get real here and use church as an example. In all too many cases, church does nothing to clear up our disease. We'll go to church and say we enjoyed the message. But in reality, we don't remember anything the pastor said. Why? Because the pastor was shooting blanks. He didn't have enough truth to impregnate us. He was unable to penetrate our subconscious, to plant a seed. He didn't even believe what *he* was saying. That's why the congregation is not being fruitful and multiplying!

This is how the Spirit summarized it for me: When people go to church, it's just like "hooking up" with a casual-sex partner. Why do we hook up? Because we want to feel good. In a casual-sex scenario, we lay there, "get the feel-good," then get up with nothing but a wet behind! It's the same with church. We'll talk about how good the service and the message were — "Ooooh, I felt the *Spirit*." That's basically the equivalent of bragging on a sexual partner, "Girl, he came and put it *down*!" You felt good at the time, but then, what did you get? What kind of connection, what kind of exchange actually happened? Or *was* there a connection? Even sexual partners who are supposedly committed to each other simply go about their relationship in the physical sense; there's not a real connection. This ties in with the Scriptural admonition to not be "unequally yoked" (2 Cor. 6:14). When you're yoked with the right person, you are in spiritual alignment; you should be able to come together and create some greatness. But if you're not equally yoked, you're going to struggle. You're going to tarry. You're going to work by the sweat of your brow. You're going to be angry. (You're going to be looking for somebody to come save you. I repeat: Nobody is coming to save you! You've got to save yourself.)

On the other hand, some of us make the mistake of refusing to have our subconscious penetrated by a messenger who doesn't meet our expectations of what that messenger should look like. For instance, I tell people, "When you sit in my presence and I bring you a word, you're going to get pregnant. Do not discount me just because I happen to be a woman." Our spirit beings have no gender. They've tried to tell women they can't preach; that it's only a man that can do so. But I can be all things to all people at all times, according to the Spirit that is in me. So, you can sit in front of me and I can give you a word. And because my conscious and my subconscious are in alignment, I can put a word in you, impregnate you and leave you wondering, *How in the world did I give birth to this?*

Again, take these genders away and we are spirit beings. Take away these titles of mother, daughter, father, son, etc.; we are spirit beings. And those earthly titles can be subdivided into different types. My mother and father were spirit beings used by God to produce me biologically, but who said they were the ones who had to "mother" and "father" me spiritually? Because of our flesh, we limited our existence — and our expectations — to the ones who gave birth to us. For me, that resulted in a whole lot of internal suffering because my mom wasn't the mom I thought she should be. I didn't realize that the Spirit knows what we need and that if we are open to it, God will send us someone to benefit us as a spiritual mother or father. But if we're stuck to our traditional understanding of the title — if we believe our biological and spiritual parent has to be one and the same — we're going to miss the blessing.

And this is why our spiritual seeds have not been watered. Our mothers and fathers carried us according to the flesh. The spiritual part of us lies dormant. It takes a spiritual person to awaken the spirit. That's why when Mary, who was pregnant with Jesus, visited her cousin Elizabeth, who was pregnant with John the Baptist, Elizabeth's baby leaped in the womb:

Now at this time Mary arose and went in a hurry to the hill country, to a city of Judah, and entered the house of Zacharias and greeted Elizabeth.

When Elizabeth heard Mary's greeting, the baby leaped in her womb; and Elizabeth was filled with the Holy Spirit. And she cried out with a loud voice and said, "Blessed are you among women, and blessed is the fruit of your womb! And how has it happened to me, that the mother of my Lord would come to me? For behold, when the sound of your greeting reached my ears, the baby leaped in my womb for joy. And blessed is she who believed that there would be a fulfillment of what had been spoken to her by the Lord." (Luke 1:39-45, NASB)

Elizabeth essentially said, "When I was in your presence, my baby leaped, because there's something in you that resonates with something in me." This represents connection.

Jesus' parable of the prodigal son, found in Luke 15:11-24, demonstrates how we may miss that connection due to the flesh ... but it's never too late to gain it:

And He said, "A man had two sons. The younger of them said to his father, 'Father, give me the share of the estate that falls to me.' So he divided his wealth between them. And not many days later, the younger son gathered everything together and went on a journey into a distant country, and there he squandered his estate with loose living. Now when he had spent everything, a severe famine occurred in that country, and he began to be impoverished. So he went and hired himself out to one of the citizens of that country, and he sent him into his fields to feed swine. And he would have gladly filled his stomach with the pods that the swine were eating, and no one was giving anything to him. But when he came to his senses, he said, 'How many of my father's hired men have more than enough bread, but I am dying here with hunger! I will get up and go to my father, and will say to him, "Father, I have sinned against heaven, and in your sight; I am no longer worthy to be called your son; make me as one of your hired men."' So he got up and came to his father. But while he was still a long way off, his father saw him and felt compassion for him, and ran and embraced him and kissed him. And the son said to him, 'Father, I have sinned against heaven and in your sight; I am no longer worthy to be called your son.' But the father said to his slaves, 'Quickly bring out the best robe and put it on him, and put a ring on his hand and sandals on his feet; and bring the fattened calf, kill it, and let us eat and celebrate; for this son of mine was dead and has come to life again; he

was lost and has been found.' And they began to celebrate. (NASB)

In this parable, you've got a younger son who asked his father for his inheritance early. His father granted the request. This young man then went off to a distant place, partied and squandered everything he had, then found himself in poverty when his new home was struck by famine. Reduced to caring for pigs, the young man came to his senses and realized that he needed to go home. The parable indicates a physical home, but in reality, he was coming back into oneness with himself. He realized that what he desired was not out there in the world. It was at home.

What did the Prodigal Son's father do, once he returned home? Welcomed him with open arms ... ordered fine clothes for him and a celebration dinner in his honor. What does our Heavenly Father do when we come back to Him? He welcomes and celebrates us.

There's more to the story, as we see in verses 25-30:

Now his older son was in the field, and when he came and approached the house, he heard music and dancing. And he summoned one of the servants and began inquiring what these things could be. And he said to him, 'Your brother has come, and your father has killed the fattened calf because he has received him back safe and sound.' But he became angry and was not willing to go

in; and his father came out and began pleading with him. But he answered and said to his father, 'Look! For so many years I have been serving you and I have never neglected a command of yours; and yet you have never given me a young goat, so that I might celebrate with my friends; but when this son of yours came, who has devoured your wealth with prostitutes, you killed the fattened calf for him.' (NASB)

The other son, once he finds out what all the commotion is about, gets angry and sulks. When his father asks what's wrong, he's like, "Dad, I've toed the line all these years and you never made all this fuss over me. My loser brother parties his money away, comes back and you lay out the red carpet." How many times have we grumbled — "I go to church and work in the church faithfully, but I don't feel fulfilled." Look. Camping out in church, volunteering for everything from the choir to the usher board, is acting according to the flesh. You're *doing* (God's work). You're not *being* (God's child). You're not at oneness with yourself; you're looking to the external.

Jesus said in Matthew 6:33 to "seek ye first the kingdom of God, and his righteousness; and all these things [our needs] shall be added unto you" (KJV). So, we seek to find the truth of who we are, and if we believe Matthew 6:33 and seek God first, then all else will be added unto us. Now we are unlimited spiritual beings. But as I indicated above, we have been limiting ourselves by *doing*, rather than *being*: "I'm gonna do church. I'm gonna do ministry. I'm gonna do business. I'm gonna do, do, do, do, do." But when we crucify the flesh, when we come into the truth of who we are (spiritual beings having a human experience), we will see the manifestation of all the things God says are ours.

Now everybody desires relationships. That's why so many people are willing to stay in unhealthy ones. For these people, the journey to being healed must begin with them letting go of what they think they know and realizing they are who God created them to be. But they can't excel, because they're tied to all these fleshly ideas, thoughts and perceptions. Detachment *has* to take place. What I realized, in my case, is that I had a lot of mind attachments … mind attachments about what my mama should be; what my daddy should be; what the church should be. All that is just bondage.

In Genesis 19 in the Old Testament, Lot's wife ended up a pillar of salt. When Lot and his family fled Sodom and Gomorrah, which God was destroying, Lot's wife looked back, despite having been warned not to do so. It would seem that she had mind attachments.

Mind attachments will stop you right in your tracks. Say you are led to start some great work. But then, here come the mind attachments — *I wonder what my husband is going to think. I wonder what my daughter is going to think. I wonder what my church is going to think.* Look, we're not here for people; we're here for God. But it's because of our mind attachments that we'll think, *Oh, if I do this, I'm going to fail.* That means you're trusting in your flesh. You already know that your flesh is going to stop you every time. When are you going to cut the cord?

Again, as it is in the natural, so it is in the spirit. When a woman gives birth, what has to happen for the baby to be separated from the mama? The umbilical cord must be cut. In the spirit, you have created all these attachments! In order for you to really be birthed, you've got to cut the cord. That's the real rebirth ... having no attachments to these things of the world. You go to that ascended place, you sit at the right hand of the Father, and you have everything He says you can have. (More about rebirth in the next chapter.)

Unfortunately, as I stated before, you'll get caught up in *doing* — "I'd better do this/that." Especially in relationships: You want to tell the other person what they can or can't do. You can't control a grown person. What you *can* do is choose. If that person's decisions and choices work for you, fine. If they don't, you need only detach and choose again! But no ... you stay in the relationship and try to make that person into something they don't want to be.

When you do this to your relationship partner, it causes their suffering. You are trying to put chains on that free spiritual being to which you're connected. Your manipulation of your partner doesn't last, because your partner tried according to the flesh to be the person you wanted, and therefore did not make enough of a connection to remain that person in season and out of season. Ultimately, you are the one suffering … because *you're* supposed to be a free spiritual being.

We'll get mad at a spouse for committing adultery, but we don't realize in the spirit, we've been adulteresses — we were supposed to be married to Christ, but we've married our job, or some other role we've taken on in the natural. Again, all the things we experience in the natural are designed for us to tie them to the Spirit. We won't cultivate or protect a healthy spiritual relationship … but we'll protect that earthly, fleshly, unhealthy relationship. And the Spirit of God is saying, *You disrespectful little heifer, you!* See how it works?

But what the enemy meant for bad, God turns around and uses for His good. It takes a negative and a positive to produce power. The bad that we have experienced was energy, designed for us to transmute into something positive … namely, a spiritual awakening. If we're going to be spiritually awakened, we have to be connected to people who themselves are spiritually awakened and who can spiritually awaken us as well. At some point, we should get hungry and desire more. Take a woman's desire to be intimate with a man. If that woman has matured, she doesn't want to just have sex anymore. She wants to be made love to. She's like, "I want a connection."

That's what your spirit is saying: *I want a connection.* But you're showing up and doing what they told you that you *should* do, and you're missing it. In church circles, it's said, "The Holy Spirit is a gentleman." In other words, the Spirit tells us, *When I give you the Word, I'm not going to rape you by forcing you to take it. You have to open up to receive it.*

Love isn't something that should be forced. It is a word that is demonstrated through action. It's my belief that love is life, and if we love someone the right way, it can lead them out of darkness. I believe the reason real love seems nonexistent is because we want someone to be something they're not. That "something" is based on what we did or didn't get as kids and adults. That trauma causes us to try to control love. To love someone is to accept them where they are. When communicating with one another, relationship partners keep love flowing by using words that will build each other up.

Toxic love, on the other hand, involves trying to force someone to love you rather than allowing love to develop through interaction. At no time should you be blaming someone else because you feel unloved. Love is authentic when freely given, not forced or given out of obligation. Love is authentic when you allow a person to be who they are … as they are. The reason we don't feel loved or appreciated by our partners is because we're giving from a place to get, not to create, which means we're *acting* (doing) instead of *being*. That's why our actions aren't translated, or felt, as love. We desire to be loved and accepted, but we don't give it because we don't have it. Then, we put pressure on others to give us what we don't have. This is selfish and self-centered of us.

Most of us don't know what healthy love looks or feels like. We reject one another because of our history and our need to be in control of love. Love is a free gift that doesn't have to be earned. When we give it freely, we create an atmosphere for love to return.

Also, love is a choice. When choosing to love, you must take nothing personally when your loved one appears to lash out at you. It has nothing to do with you; rather, it has to do with your loved one's past. When you're "love sick," you're going to *in*fect and *af*fect all those connected to you, causing the disease to spread. When you are love-healthy, you can help your partner, and others, become healthy.

CHAPTER EIGHT

REBIRTH

We are all spirits first. But in the natural, we are created in the image and likeness of our mom and our dad, because those are the first "gods" we experience in the earth. When they birth us, we look and act like them. Then, God tells us, "You were formed in *My* image, in *My* likeness." Our realization of this represents our *rebirth*.

Now this is where I got confused. I went to church and thought that, by simply confessing my faith in Christ, I would be born again and that would be the end of the story. It doesn't work that way. Salvation — and living life more abundantly — is a process. I was born into sin, shaped in the iniquities of my forefathers. I came into the earth realm as spirit, but in a fleshly body. In order to get back to spirit, I had to journey to my freedom, because I was birthed with everything my mama and my daddy were. Remember, I was created in their image and their likeness. My mom and my dad were unconscious. My mom had rejection and abandonment issues. My dad had a heart issue. Those are the seeds that they reproduced in me.

So, God said, "I have made a Christel in the earth." He sent me forth — we are Christ in the earth, right? When we come into this earth realm, we're supposed to change it for the better because we came to save and to set free. But we can't save anyone else, and set anyone else free, if we haven't saved ourselves. We've been looking for somebody else to save us, but it's our journey that saves us, not an individual. We are God in the earth! All the answers are within us. But if we don't do the research, we will never find it.

As my parents could only reproduce their issues in me, I could only reproduce my issues in my five children. When I looked at them through my opened eyes, I saw that I had done exactly that, especially as far as the first three were concerned.

My eldest son bore the same rejection and abandonment issues I did. He wanted a child who would love him … just as I'd wanted a child who would love me, which is why I had him. He is me all over again. He went out of one marriage right into another one, doing the exact thing his mama had done.

My second son had a closed heart. He was, by nature, a very loving, caring, compassionate young man, but he'd been hurt. When he got hurt, he withdrew himself and turned to self-medicating in various ways so that he wouldn't have to feel. That was his mama, too.

My daughter? Same thing: She chose a man over herself. She sacrificed her dreams and her goals, just like her mom once did.

God said He wouldn't leave or forsake us. Paul wrote this in 2 Corinthians 4:3: "But if our gospel be hid, it is hid to them that are lost" (KJV). It's no longer hidden to you when you're not lost. It's the same with the life realizations the gospel spawns — those realizations by which our conscious and unconscious come into alignment. These children I had birthed held the clues I needed to not only save *my* soul but save *theirs*. So now, I am looking at the mirror of the energetic soul tie that I birthed. They were created in the image and likeness of what I thought, what I believed, how I saw myself. I'd seen myself as not good enough. And I saw all my negative attributes in my kids. I looked at them like, *Oh my goodness! I really did this to my babies!* Nobody had taught me any better.

When I got the revelations about my rejection and abandonment issues and my tendency to choose a man over myself, I was able to go and share these revelations with my mother. She'd had nobody to help her see it.

So, God's message to her was this: *I will send forth one who is the image of you to show you how to save yourself.* My mom has entered her 70s, and as I receive a revelation, I share with her. These revelations are helping her to get free.

My children, all along, were leading the way for me. Because of my old subconscious programming, I hadn't seen it. As I related in my last book, my daughter and I had a conversation that caused me to realize that if I didn't do something different, she was going to do the same unhealthy things I'd done. My kids were clues to what I needed to heal inside of me.

After that weekend I spent alone, I went to my office and this overwhelming feeling of gratitude came over me. I began thanking and praising God and speaking life over my children. It wasn't an hour later that I got a call. My second son, who lives in another city, had been in a car accident; he had hit a pole. He had been doing some things he shouldn't have been doing. The woman who called to give me the news begged me not to tell my son that she had told me.

After the call, I sat down and the Spirit spoke to me: *If you had not obeyed Me and gotten off to yourself to hear Me speak to you, your son would have had to become a sacrifice for you to get the message.*

Every time I think about this, I say, "Thank You, God!" This life isn't about me; it's about what God wants to do through me. Had I bowed to my flesh … had I refrained from getting off to myself, and thereby hearing from God, because I didn't want to hurt my husband's feelings … had I not stood in my truth … I would have lost my son. There was a spiritual thing going on here, not a fleshly thing. *Obedience is better than sacrifice,* God said.

When I say this hit me in my chest, I mean it! I boo-hooed and started thanking and praising God all over again. I was so excited.

And then God said, *I told you, Christel, that if you make your bed in Hell, I'm there. Your son is crying out for his soul to be saved. Go get him.*

I called him and said, "I'm coming to get you."

"What's wrong?" he asked.

"Nothing's wrong," I said. "I just think you need your mama and your mama needs you."

He said, "OK."

Usually, he would have argued or at least asked, "What do you mean, Mama?" or, "I've got to work, Mama." But he just said "OK," because the spirit in him needed what I had received. I can't take my son somewhere I haven't been, so I had to deal with the matters of my heart. I knew that when he arrived home, I would be able to help him save himself, because I had saved *my*self.

My eldest son and my daughter, meanwhile, had already begun doing their soul work. Recently, my eldest son called me and said, "Mama I had to leave," referring to his marriage.

"You left?" I asked.

"Yes," he answered. "I'm not healthy. I can never give my wife what she desires. And I've been trying to give everybody else what I never gave me. I'm tired of being unhappy."

Earlier I made mention of an energetic soul tie. These scenarios, in which my children's lives became a reflection of my sickness and are now becoming a reflection of my healing, were enabled due to energetic soul ties. I don't have to physically be with my kids, because they are energetically connected to me. As I reverse the issues in me, the issues are automatically reversing in them. I don't have to have a conversation with them. I don't even have to be in the same vicinity as they are. My work (on myself) is transforming the DNA that's been handed down.

At the time I began writing this book, my second son was the one remaining child who had yet to begin his soul work. He had completely withdrawn himself from me. Really, his soul was calling out for connection ... the same thing my soul had once cried out for. When I was a child, communication between my mother and me usually consisted of her asking, "Is your room clean?" "Did you do your homework?" "Did you fold those clothes?" I don't recall being asked or told anything that represented an emotional connection. As a result, I didn't know what this felt like. And when I became a mother, I simply performed the outward duties mamas performed ... going to work and providing for my children.

As I'd promised, I went to get my son. I was planning to spend a week embracing a little boy who didn't get the love and attention he needed. It was to be a week for me to connect with him.

The first night he was home, we sat and talked.

"Son, I know you, as a man, would never have called and said, 'Mama, I need you,'" I told him. "The little boy in you is crying out for me to give him what I didn't know how to give when you were growing up."

"What are you talking about?" he asked.

"Son, you desire to be loved for who you are, not for what you can do. You desire to be heard and understood. You stay silent about the things that have hurt you the most."

Tears began to roll down his face. "How did you know?" he asked.

We embraced.

"You are me and I am you," I answered. "This is the reason I am doing my soul work, and why I brought you home. My children are my why. I don't want y'all to struggle like I did, and if I don't do my work, I can't take y'all somewhere I haven't been. I refuse to quit. You, son, are worth fighting for.

"I brought you home to love on you, to hear you, to make you aware that nothing is wrong with you. You are not alone. I'm here for you."

He cried and cried. His words to me at the end of that evening were "Mom, I really, *really* needed this."

A couple weeks after returning home, he called me and said, "I am so grateful to have you as my mom. And since I've been home, this is the most peace I have had in a long, long time. I love you, Mom. Thank you."

Emotional fulfillment is wanted and needed by our children. Because I never had it, I could neither teach nor give it. Thank God, it wasn't too late!

To summarize how my issues affected my children:

I created them in my image and likeness, according to my flesh.

Seed 1 became a reflection of my need to be loved and accepted.

Seed 2 had a closed heart due to hurt. He sought comfort and solace in the wrong places.

Seed 3 sacrificed her dreams because she lacked self-love and believed she wasn't enough.

Seed 4 is naturally gifted, excels in everything he does and has very high expectations of himself.

Seed 5 has a desire to be accepted and loved and will sacrifice himself for the sake of making others happy. He has a heart to serve the less fortunate.

In order for me to experience my rebirth, I had to heal all these aspects of myself to clean up my bloodline. It is through the death of my flesh that my children and grandchildren will have life more abundant. I took our sins/unbelief to the cross; now they will know me, and themselves, by the Spirit. IT IS FINISHED.

CHAPTER NINE

BLIND (SELF-) FAITH

As part of my journey to my rebirth, I did a spiritual autopsy and found the cause of the death of my former self to be rejection, abandonment and heart failure. I'm convinced that the reason society has the problems it does is because there's so much rejection and abandonment, and there's no heart connection. This is the sickness of the world. This is the energy our society holds: *Nobody loves me. Nobody accepts me as I am.* And because we have been so concerned about what we didn't get, we have not taken time to look and realize that we haven't even *connected* with people, not even those we birthed into this earth realm. We have not connected with our children in a way in that would help them to live. Therefore, they are out here in pursuit of what they never got at home. The cycle has continued in all our lives, because the energetic soul tie, biological soul tie, DNA, generational curse — whatever you want to call it — is still drawing those same experiences. In my case, nobody helped me see that it was *me* rejecting me. My soul was out here wandering, because I hadn't loved and accepted me.

Again, we are taught that the only way to save our souls is to accept Jesus Christ as our Lord and Savior, but I came to understand that the story didn't end with my being saved from hell. I had to complete that abundant-life picture; I had to love and accept me. I had to believe I was worthy of divine love. I had to believe I could experience that type of connection.

We encounter the *personality* of another person, but not the *Christ* in the person. The Christ in the person never gets an opportunity to manifest. So, we just exist on this one plane ... never, ever ascending into who God created us to be. We are two parts. When you go to hell — to the deep, dark places of your soul — you get the key to free yourself and experience heaven on earth. So that's what I did; I took the journey to get the key. I went to hell to free myself. Christ, who gave His life for us, has already done what He had come to do: "He that believeth on me, the works that I do shall he do also; and greater works than these shall he do; because I go unto my Father" (John 14:12, KJV). Jesus has shown you the way. What are you going to do?

Literally, this is the journey to me ... my coming into my healing. I was born in the image and likeness of my earthly father. I had to die to that. And I had to be born again of the spirit. Now, being born again of the spirit, I had to peel away all those aspects of myself. I had to take the journey. I had to separate the truth from the lie. And then I had to choose love.

This is the declaration I made: *I choose love; I choose me.* The Word says that God is love. Well, I am God in the earth. I choose love; I choose me. I was not looking for anybody else to do it. I did it for myself.

That right there has given me the liberty to declare that I can now live a life of no limits, no boundaries. Why? Because I took the limits off. As long as I was simply operating in this fleshly realm, I was limited to fleshly things. That changed when I took the limits off and opened up my heart. Remember, we are spiritual beings, having a human experience. If we're spiritual beings, that means there are no limits for us. We've seen the Biblical mention of the streets of gold. Well, when we are truly born again, life looks like that. We can have whatever we like! The journey to my healing wasn't easy, but it wasn't about me. Even Jesus, in the garden of Gethsemane just before His crucifixion, asked if this bitter cup could pass Him by. But then,

He acknowledged that "it's not about Me, God. It's about what You're doing through me."

I tell people this all the time: When it was "according to Crystal's will," I would cuss you out and tell you what I wasn't going to do: "No, I'm not going to love you. I'm not going to be there for you." But the *spirit* of Christel knows that it's not about me. It's about what God wants to do through me. God wants to love through me. In order for me to love like that, I had to love *me* like that.

Loving and accepting myself was how I saved my soul. It was how I freed the little girl within me. She was still playing her role out in me with those temper tantrums over the things she hadn't gotten and was still crying out for. Life had happened fast for me. I became a mother at the age of 15, and I skipped a lot of stuff. Well, we can't skip the processes that are necessary to our healthy development. In order for my soul to be healed and whole, there were places I had to go back and revisit. I had to gather those pieces of my soul and put them back together so that I could be delivered into the life that was created for me ... not the life I was delivered into.

CHAPTER TEN

THE DIVORCE IS FINAL

*T*here is no going back: I have divorced my old way of living. I have positioned myself to create and experience new life. All old things must pass away in order for me to experience the new. I just made room for all the greatness in store for me.

Life is the great teacher. Looking back on my former marriage, for instance, I realize that my physical union was a reflection of my lack of commitment and dedication to myself. I wanted to be married, but never made the commitment internally. I didn't know *how* to do so. My heart was in one place and my mind was in another. I believe that's why Proverbs 23:7 says that "as [a man] thinketh in his heart, so is he" (KJV). I thought that no one loved me. To be honest, I never saw *anyone* have a healthy relationship with themselves.

Now how did we learn about romantic relationships? By what we saw and what we heard. I don't remember having any conversations that addressed loving one's self. We just saw what was presented to us as ideal images, and we went from there. And when I say "we," I'm including the Body of Christ … the church. We blame it on the devil. It's not the devil, doggone it. It's US!

We have to work on *us* to get *us* together. But nobody wants to take responsibility for doing that. And it's because it's not been laid out in a way that people understand it. Everybody wants the bells and whistles. They want to get married. They want to walk down the aisle. The man wants the bachelor party. The woman wants the bachelorette party. They want all the external things, but they have not made that commitment internally. At one point, as I reflected on marriage, I had to ask myself: *Christel, have you made vows to yourself? Have you promised to honor, love, respect, cherish yourself? How can you go to the altar and give somebody what you don't have?*

When you marry, then attempt to give your spouse what you lack, you've started your marriage out at a deficit! You have holes in your cup! Let's say you're a man who has issues with women, and you've never dealt with those issues. Then, a woman shows up in your life … a woman who could be that very woman to fill your cup. If your cup has holes in it, you'll never be able to recognize her for who she is, or why God put her in your life. Every time she pours herself into your cup, there's a leak! And what happens to the person who's pouring herself into her partner's holey cup? She starts to feel unappreciated. Nobody helped her to understand that she was pouring into a cup that lacked the capacity to hold what she was pouring. So, she withdraws.

Everybody wants to be loved and accepted, but what we should be giving, we withhold because we take things personally.

I now know that when somebody's behavior triggers me, this issue is something that needs to be exposed and released. That person is not doing anything *to* me. Rather, the situation has happened *for* me. But if I carry a victim mentality, I'm going to see it as happening *to* me, and I'm going to get angry at the person I believe has wronged me. In such a case, I'm not a victim; I've become a volunteer. I signed up for my own predicament.

God gave us free will … and all too often, we'll choose to give our power to somebody else, become frustrated with that person, and wonder why the blessings are not flowing to us. It's because we are living a lie! Until we face our truth, we'll never find our power. The relationship starts with us! That's getting back to the root. Look again at Matthew 6:33, where Jesus says to "seek ye first the kingdom of God, and His righteousness; and all these things shall be added unto you" (KJV). Where is the kingdom of God? It is within us! God is telling us, *When you seek and find the truth of who I created you to be, the things you need will be added unto you. But I can't give you the blessing if you're not being who I created you to be.*

So, the struggle you experience in your everyday life may well be resolved by the answer to the question: In what area are you not being authentic?

The Spirit is always convicting us, but we don't listen. Our spirit is innocent, just like that of a child. (Matthew 18:3 says that we have to repent and become as little children to enter the Kingdom of Heaven.) But because we're, say, 40-50 years of age, we believe we're supposed to know how to run things ourselves. The Holy Spirit, the driver of that innocent, childlike nature inside us, is saying, *Turn left.* But our grown, think-we-know-it-all self is saying, "Uh-uh, I'm going to go right!"

You have to learn to submit to the Holy Spirit, the Divine Guide for your spirit ... the essence of who you are. When you do, you'll stop getting your tail whooped! Everything you're experiencing is self-inflicted! If you don't like what you're getting, you've got to do something different. As the saying goes, insanity is doing the same thing over and over again, expecting different results.

Granted, it's uncomfortable to walk this walk. Many people are unwilling to turn away from what they have known. That 1999 science fiction movie *The Matrix* highlights this issue: People preferred to live the illusory life, the fake reality they'd been plugged into by predatory machines, rather than actual reality. How many generations have we seen do the same things? You know what's down that road. When are you going to do something different?

You may be walking in your failure, thinking it's too *late* to do something different. You've reached an age where you believe you're supposed to have "gotten it." You don't have it, so you're walking around with your head down. Honey, that's just the devil discouraging you from taking responsibility for your life. God told me, *I gave you all power. I gave you an example, in the beginning, with Adam. I gave Adam the animals and said, "Adam, that animal is going to be what you call it." I give you situations all day long, Christel. You have the power to call them … to say what will happen.*

God is telling all of us the same thing: *It's going to be what you call it.* But what will we do? We'll call it what we *don't* want … and then get angry because *we got what we were thinking.* We'll give our power away instead of using it — "having a form of godliness, but denying the power thereof" (2 Timothy 3:5, KJV).

Many of us went to our old, traditional churches and learned *religion.* What did religion do? I'll tell you what it *didn't* do: It didn't show us how to look to the power within. When I took a really close look at the story of Christ, I had to thank God anew for my Big Brother, Jesus. He is my Mentor. The Scripture says that "the Word became flesh." And He showed me that I would have to crucify my flesh: *You're going to have to die to what you think you know. You're going to have to resurrect it as the Way, the Truth and the Life.* How are you going to lead someone to life and show them the way if you're not living your truth?

Yes ... in order to save your soul, you have to accept Christ. Well, where is Christ? He is one with us, therefore, it's the love and acceptance of self that completes the soul-saving process. But we have limited it to, again, something external. When you *really* love and accept yourself, you save your soul. It's complete. We are commanded to love the Lord with all our heart, soul, strength and mind (Deuteronomy 6:5; Matthew 22:37; Luke 10:27). People limit God to the external, but God is not separate from us; He is one with us. Jesus, after stating that loving God with your all was the first and greatest commandment, went on to highlight the second most important commandment — to love your neighbor as yourself (Matthew 22:39). Why would He say that the second commandment is like unto the first? Because He was saying, *Love YOU with all your heart, mind and soul;* then *you can love your neighbor as yourself.* As I've pointed out multiple times now, you can't give somebody something you don't have.

I once heard Holton Buggs, network-marketing expert and chairman and chief executive officer of Ibuumerang. com, make this point: The rich say they're lucky and we'll say we're blessed. The rich *are* lucky because they are Laboring Under Correct Knowledge — their LUCK. But we'll say we're blessed, and we're broke. Why? Because we lack the proper knowledge. Buggs pointed out that everything has evolved except for how we make our money. We used to have big, heavy tube TVs with rabbit ears; now we have flat-screen "smart" TVs. We used to have clunky house phones that were plugged into special wall jacks; now we've got these smartphones that do everything for us. We used to listen to music on vinyl records and 8-track tape; now, we listen to it on MP4 files. Yet, we still think we've got to work 40 hours a week for 40 years, then retire on 40 percent of our pay … not enough for us to live on. It's the system, it's the perpetuating cycle, and it's why poverty still exists, Buggs said. We're still laboring under incorrect knowledge.

We need to get the right knowledge, especially in terms of relationships. We've been taught how to *do* relationships. I knew in my mind how to treat someone in a way that would convey love; in other words, I knew how to *do* love. But I didn't know how to *be* love. What is God? God *is* love. I didn't know how to be love … and to be love is to be Christel.

What comes from the heart reaches the heart. If I'm being me, then when I minister to you, I'm going to minister to your heart. But if I'm *doing* it, then it's an act. It's external. This is why there's a lack of connection. Everybody has become human *doers* instead of human *beings*. God didn't create us to be doers. He created us to be. But society puts value in what we do. If we don't cook, if we don't clean, if we don't wash dishes, if we don't go to work, if we don't pay the bills — all those external things — we are seen as having no worth. But what about the things within?

When you ask people, "What do you bring to your relationships?", they can't even answer. This is where we lack connection. We'll subscribe to illusions of connection. For instance, we'll believe that just because we've got a piece of paper, we're married. No! Love is supposed to be a continual flow. I'm not supposed to have to force you to love me the way I *think* you're supposed to love me. When I'm operating from a place of being who God created me to be, I can show up in your life and you don't have to ask me anything. The love is going to flow naturally.

I thought my first book, *The Journey to My Healing*, was all about having a right relationship with one's self: Because you heal you, you heal your family, you heal your relationships, you heal your business, you heal your body; you heal everything. But God got me in that gym and said, *THIS is the journey to your healing.* "This" was in me, but I was, I guess you could say, emotionally stuck. My desire for something different in my life brought a full understanding and realization of why I was where I was.

Third John 2 says, "Beloved, I wish above all things that thou mayest prosper and be in health, even as thy soul prospereth" (KJV). I wanted prosperity and I wanted good health. But until I did my soul work, none of those things could happen. So, I was stuck in my emotional trauma. I was on life support and I had to unplug. Now, it's all about Christel. I told someone that I go to the gym so much now that when I don't go, I get angry. Exercise is something I'm giving *me*. It's like being in a new relationship with that special guy. Every minute, you're like, "Can I just go see him? Can I talk to him? I've got to hook up with my Boo!" When you fall in love with yourself, your desire is not for somebody else to give you what you want; your desire is to give it to yourself. If you give it to yourself, nobody can take it from you. I love my husband, but he doesn't complete me. My cup is full. He adds to what I have; he runs my cup over. But he is not filling my cup. I am.

When we've got that type of understanding, we can have healthy relationships. But no, we've looked outside ourselves and decided that another person is going to change our lives for the better. Because that person "let us down," we're frustrated.

I compare my transformation to that of the main character in the 1993 movie *Sankofa*. In this film, a haughty, Eurocentric black model is on a photo shoot in Ghana when she's transported from her 20th-century world to the antebellum South, where she is a slave abused by her master. By the time she is restored to her modern-day world, she's had a big attitude adjustment. She now knows where she's come from. That knowledge has freed her and has allowed her to go forward in her freedom. "Sankofa" is an African word in the Akan language; it means looking back at, and learning from, one's past in order to go into the future. I feel that the word sankofa and its symbol — a bird looking back, dropping an egg from its mouth — embodies my message. As I watched that movie, I cried. "God, I see what You're doing in me and through me," I said. "My feet are pointing forward, but You've got me looking back, and now the future is in my mouth." That's my tattoo. That's my signature.

Then, here comes *Harriet*, the movie about Harriet Tubman released in late 2019. It's a universal message: Once you get free, you've got to go back and free those who are still enslaved. That's what ministry is about. You've got to *get* free if you're going to *set somebody else* free. We're still walking around here *pretending* we are free. We're dressing up our bondage. But I've been chosen to break that. God and the ancestors have summoned me.

The divorce is final.

CHAPTER ELEVEN

I FOUND THE ONE
I WAS LOOKING FOR
(AND IT WAS ME)

*T*he beginning of my relationship with the gym marked the beginning of the friendship I developed with myself. Eventually, the real commitment took place. I stopped allowing situations and circumstances to distract me from coming into unity with *me*. I have returned to my first love, the love of myself ... the Christ in me. I can have the courtship, the marriage ceremony, the honeymoon. I can have with myself all the things relationships go through in the natural ... but in this case, tied into the spirit.

I was looking past the mirror for what was right in front of me all along. I looked to a man to give me what I hadn't given myself. When I started giving it to myself, I realized *I* was the one I'd been looking for! Now, I can draw from *me* what I desire. I had to find it in *me* if I was going to find it in somebody else. What we can't identify in us, we're not going to see in anyone else. We'll look at another person and say, "You ain't doing this," "You ain't doing that." Well, it's because we're not releasing that energy ourselves.

I had to become healed and whole if I was going to have a healed and whole husband. I had to work on the things I deemed negative. My husband said, "Look, you've got all these ideas. You said you were going to create this, that and the other, but you're not doing anything." When I sat back and thought about it, I had to tell myself, "Christel, you *aren't* doing anything." I remember apologizing to him once, because there was a point in our marriage when I accused him of not desiring me. The truth was, I didn't desire myself. As women, we often put the status of our desirability on a man to give to us. And, we haven't given it to ourselves! Do we know what makes us happy? Do we know what makes us tick? Do we know, really, what satisfies us? Most women that I mentor do not know. They are acting according to what they have heard and seen. They have never opened themselves up to really feel what's right for them.

I believe we are shifting into a dispensation in which people are tired of the external. They're like, "God, I want to *feel* your presence." We go to church to experience God's presence. The people who actually feel Him do so not just because the pastor is doing a good job of conveying the Word; it's because they've opened their hearts. Most of us have our walls up, so we don't experience *anything*. We just show up for the churchy version of that wet behind we end up with after a lustful romp in bed. (Well, in church, it's a wet face!) It's just a temporary "feel-good." But now, people are beginning to want the real thing — "I want connection, God. I want healthy relationships — spiritual relationships."

We can provide those desired spiritual relationships. We can call people from that dead place when we are truly alive and at one with ourselves. In the 11th chapter of Luke, Jesus went to the tomb of Lazarus, who had been dead for four days. He commanded: "Lazarus, come forth!" and raised Lazarus from the dead. Now, if Jesus Himself was dead, He couldn't have called *anybody* forth! If we are living, we can cause others to live. We can tell them that it's OK for them for take their grave clothes off. The reason Christ was able to call Lazarus forth was because of the power and the oneness within Him.

When I had my Xhale to Xcel women's empowerment weekend, I had women coming from Philadelphia,

New York, New Jersey. One lady drove from North Carolina to Atlanta, caught a Megabus to Mississippi, then caught a ride from Mississippi to Arkansas. God said, *Christel, the gift I have given you has caused the people to come forward.*

I said, "God you are so strategic! It was no accident that you named me Christel, or CHRIST TELL." He knew I was going to tell about the Christ — the True and Living Christ.

Know that if you *pretend* to be alive and at one with yourself, you will fall on your face when you try to impart into someone else. You can't just tell others what you heard somebody else say. If you have not walked that thing out yourself, your words are not going to penetrate another's subconscious to bring forth a different harvest in that person's life. What have you walked in? Jesus walked His story! We are Christ in the earth; why are we not telling stories that can help bring forth a different harvest in the lives of the people? Jesus has shown us an example of what to do!

And the truth is being hidden in plain sight. In Mark 8:18, Jesus asked His disciples, "Having eyes, do you not see? And having ears, do you not hear? And do you not remember?" (NASB) God is telling us, *You can't see what I'm trying to show you — the spiritual truth about what you're experiencing. You're choosing to see it according to your senses when it's bigger than that. You're hearing with your fleshly ears, but you're not hearing with the Spirit, so you don't under-stand what I'm trying to tell you about your life. You're miss-ing it.* That's why our lives are so unsatisfying. Meanwhile, we're still hoping that "God's gonna do it," or wishing He would. Once again: Nobody is coming to save you from your misery. God has already equipped you to save your-self!

When I started to operate in the new mindset God gave me, He told me, *Christel, you are the current that creates the currency.* He was saying, *When you understand that you are an unlimited, infinite spiritual being — when you believe that, when you become one with that — there is nothing you can't manifest. The reason lack is in your life is because you have not believed that the you I created you to be is enough.*

Now, as I contemplate the letters of my name, I can see the positive attributes that I have found in me.

C. Conscious

H. Happy

R. Resilient

I. Intelligent

S. Seeker

T. Tenacious

E. Empowering

L. Light

The title of this chapter references Song of Solomon 3:4 — "I found him whom my soul loveth" — as well as a popular wedding slogan built on that Scripture: "I have found the one whom my soul loves." I sought one outside myself, and I didn't find fulfillment. I have now found the one my soul loves … me.

EPILOGUE

I must add that the type of spiritual teaching I've revealed in this book is not welcome among the traditional-minded. I was trying to share my revelations with a woman who kept asking me, "Now how do you tie that to the Word of God?" And God said, *See, a person with that mindset is not going to receive what you're saying.* She wanted someone to come at her in that old, traditional package she's used to. My question is: Why are you going to keep doing what hasn't worked?

Other religious people come at me when they hear me share these truths. Everything I'm teaching is a spiritual download. But I'm not going to give you theologian talk. I'm going to give you Christel-lations! This is according to the truth that God spoke to me. Truth stands on its own. I'm not going to be your teacher and hold your hand. Because God gave this to me as a result of what I went through, it's going to touch your heart. I don't have to sit and find a Scripture to back up every sentence that comes out of my mouth. I'm not that teacher.

God is teaching me how to answer my critics. When He first spoke these things to me, I argued a bit. "The principle works," I said. "But if You haven't taught me how to break up this fallow ground, it won't make any sense for me to say anything. And I'm not going to tell my kids or anybody else to keep *saying* the same thing they've been hearing in the church. That is a dysfunctional system. There are people 50 and 60 years old sitting in church right now, angry. They're still 'naming it and claiming it.' They've got nothing, and they haven't asked themselves why. But You're trying to tell me to keep teaching them."

God drew me to 3 John 2, the Scripture I mentioned in Chapter Ten: "Beloved, I wish above all things that thou mayest prosper and be in health, even as thy soul prospereth." I NEEDED TO DO SOME SOUL WORK IF I WAS GOING TO EXPERIENCE PROSPERITY.

"But God, you told me to name it and claim it," I protested. "You told me to just confess and I was going to be saved and that was it."

But my journey didn't end with confession. There was some soul work I had to do. It's according to my faith and according to what I seek that what I desire will be done to unto me. I can name and claim something all day long, but if I don't believe what I speak, I'm going to get nothing. I've got to learn to love myself. I've got to see myself through the eyes of God — not my experiences or my circumstance — so that, when a good word comes to me, I'm able to receive it. I cannot receive it if I'm stuck in my trauma.

Jesus said in Luke 23:34, as He was being crucified, "Father, forgive them, for they know not what they do" (KJV). He asked for forgiveness for people who were basically stuck in their tradition/trauma. If I hurt you, it's because I am not seeing with my spiritual eyes or hearing with my spiritual ears; therefore, I don't understand. How about you loving me and helping me to see correctly, rather than condemning me? Not only did Jesus pray, "Father, forgive them, for they know not what they do," but, in the garden of Gethsemane prior to being arrested, He prayed and told God, "Not my will, but thine, be done" (Luke 22:42, KJV). What He was saying was, "Now according to my flesh, I should whip the behinds of the ones who are about to crucify Me. But, according to the Spirit, I'm going to forgive them, for they don't know what they're really doing."

According to this flesh, "If you wrong me, you ain't right." And we focus on what we *don't* want. We don't realize that we're *creating* more of what we don't want. I'm guilty of it. I was focused on my debt. I was focused on my bills. I was focused on all the things I didn't have. And as a result, I was creating more of what I didn't want. My focus wasn't on the fact that God created me to be a *solution*. I was focused on my problems, so I kept creating more problems!

When you have expectations, you have an attachment, so that means the Spirit can't flow. You've already got it set in your mind that this is how things are supposed to be. And you're stuck. Look, God called us to live in the present. All we've got is this moment, right here, right now. Our next moment, our next second, is not promised to us. So, until you leave here, just stay in the flow of the Spirit! Quit worrying about the outcome of situations. Quit harboring expectations that people will be to you what you are to them. Quit actively resisting what you don't want. What you resist, you're going to draw to you, so the key to living your best life is not resistance ... just acceptance. Say to yourself, "Things are not happening *to* me, everything is happening *for* me." And I promise you — you will have no problem harboring gratitude.

I started focusing on my blessings, telling myself, "It's not as bad as it could be. I've got so much to be thankful for." If I limit my gratitude to what I see, taste, hear, smell and touch, I am *not* living life as the infinite spiritual being God created me to be! It's so much more than the tangible stuff. Before that, I'd gotten caught up ... I'd gotten tricked

… someone had slipped me a mickey and told me, "This is what so-and-so is all about."

I thought I had to have this, and that, to be happy. None of that is more fulfilling to me than empowering others. Nothing is more fulfilling to me than changing lives. And I know that when I'm upgrading a person, all that I desire will come. All those things can be added to me if I return to my first love.

All things can be added to *you*. When you come back to your first love, you come back into oneness with yourself. No greater scenario is the one where you say, "I've found her! She has been here all along. I've just been looking past her and looking to everything and everybody else." When you look in the mirror, you'll see that *that's* the one you've been looking for! And when you find her, your attitude is, "I'm not letting her go."

I'm in a place now where it doesn't matter what someone thinks of me. It doesn't even matter if they walk away. I no longer have any fear. Perfect love casts out fear (1 John 4:18), so if God's love has been made perfect in you, you don't fear anything happening *to* you; it's all happening *for* you. It's a beautiful place to be in! When I find myself thinking about what I don't have and what I should accomplish, I take a moment to say, "You know what, God? I'm grateful. I'm thankful." When you do this, you start releasing the energy of what you don't want. I remind myself,

"God created you to be a solution, Christel. Why are you focused on the problem?"

When you have a spiritual transcendence, realize that some won't relate to you. It's like having human immunodeficiency virus (HIV); they'll stay infected … just like that woman I was trying to teach and who kept coming back at me, talking religion. Well, you know what? You're going to keep your virus. You're going to keep your infection. You don't want to open yourself to seeing things a different way. There's nothing I can do about that. But again, the biggest thing for me was learning to be thankful and grateful. That helps creates more of what I want. There is no lack in me.

Society and religion have taught us that we can't be ourselves. According to others' truth, beliefs and doctrine, we have to stay inside a box. We have to be cute and proper, sharing what we know … no dancing, no cussing, no wine drinking, no "odd" behavior, no hanging out with outcasts, etc. That is so wrong. It is not our job to judge. It's our job to sit back and receive truth. (I like to have my occasional glass of wine or margarita — and have fun. And I challenge anybody to tell me I'm going to hell because of it.) If someone's truth resonates with you, what's wrong with listening to it? Try the spirit by the Spirit. Oh, and remember that Jesus didn't keep Himself inside a building. He was out working miracles.

When I had my women's conference, I told the ladies, "We've been so institutionalized, religion-ized, whatever you want to call it. Do you not know that God's gifts and calling are without repentance" (Romans 11:29)? *What are you saying, Christel?* I'm saying I'll cuss your butt out, take a shot of tequila and still pray for you to get delivered! God gives gifts without repentance! But if you look at what I'm doing and reject me because you see me as an unfit messenger, you're going to miss God. These bodies that house our spirits are just avatars. If you get caught up in what my avatar is doing, that's on you. I don't have to justify the spirit that's in me. It does that all by itself.

Really, this journey — this walk — is beautiful. It's fun when we ascend from that box in our mind. That is what limits us, trips us up. We let people put us in positions and titles. Whoever you say I am, that's who I'm going to be to you. I just need you to call me Christel, and not limit me to a title. I want you to know the fullness of me. My spirit can be all things to all people at all times. But if you box me in, I'm going to be who you say I am. Thus, I'm limited in my ability to give to you, and you are certainly limited in receiving. Let me pour out to you the way the Spirit leads me.

At the conference, which went from Friday evening to Sunday, we had karaoke, we had wine, we sang women's empowerment songs, we line-danced. We had a good time.

God said, *Christel, there is so much expectation when it come to the word 'power' and the word 'conference.' There's already a programming, a certain mindset, when it comes to what those are. I want you to tear all that down.* The ladies thought they would be following a formal agenda, but an atmosphere was created for them to be free. Women like to have an atmosphere set for them. So, I set the mood. All they had to do was come and receive. By Saturday, they were open to doing so.

What I really love is that they were from my mom's generation. The oldest one there was 65. My daughter, at 23, was the youngest. But most of the women were 40 and up. These women had never had permission to have a voice. They'd never been in an atmosphere where they could be liberated to share their truth. I'd say that 70 percent of them had been molested or touched inappropriately as girls and had never talked about it. God revealed to me that it was people of this generation who were forced to keep secrets — "Don't tell on Uncle So-and-So," "The family sticks together" — and they'd been carrying their shame all these years. I just weep for all the women who are in that generation and who are stuck because of traumas for which the only support they received was advice to "pray about it."

Not only did these women get free during the women's empowerment conference sessions; we went to the club that Saturday night! We danced and had a good time. Sunday morning, we got up and did a spiritual workout. We talked about emotions and such. Again, the beauty of it all was the freedom the women experienced. One woman had been married for 30-something years; her husband commented that "my wife hasn't been the same since she left Little Rock." It was because she'd had the opportunity to talk about the brother who had molested her. She had been stuck in her trauma. The Bible says, "confess your faults one to another" (James 5:16). She had not had an opportunity to confess this and be heard ... and validated. Before this, she'd worn a mask. I said, "Mask off this weekend, baby. Whoever you are, let her out." That's what I said all weekend — "Let her out. She wants to get free anyway. Let her out. You've been hiding her. Let her out." So, some of the ladies got *real*. When we danced, the 65-year-old got down! She'd been wanting to do this all along but had not been in an atmosphere where she could be free.

I was so overwhelmed by the liberation these women now walked in, I think I cried for two days. My heart was so full of gratitude.

Our physical bodies would die if our hearts stopped. Well, the reason Scripture says that your latter days will be greater than your former (Job 8:7) is because when you open up your heart and become reborn, the heart is rejuvenated. People always tell me, "Oh, you look so young."

It's because I open my heart to experiencing life, not just in the physical but in the spiritual. That's the heart that gives me abundant life.

Our hearts have been closed because of our experiences and our limited belief that life is just about our surroundings and circumstances. Life is so much more than that, but we've got to "go through" to get there. The way up is down. We can go to hell and get the keys!

At the time I was finishing this book, I was preparing to close my adult day care business and help others with their journeys back to themselves. I'd been asked to be a speaker for a national event in one city, making the Sweet Life presentation I do in the schools and then in the community. I also had accepted invitations to speak in other cities ... all expenses paid.

I did as Jesus invited Peter to do — step out of the boat and walk on water or, in other words, have faith. I believe the Christel that God created me to be is enough. The carnal mind would say that it's stupid to walk away from a business, to walk away from the things one depends on. But my hope and trust are no longer in man. My hope and trust are in God and who He created me to be. I'm going to use the gift God has given me to impact, empower and inspire the world.

In Genesis 12, God told Abraham, "Go. I'm going to show you a land, and I will tell you more as you go." So, I'm out here like him, as well as like Peter on the water. It's my faith, and the belief in myself, that empowered me to do that. I know God is not going to leave me out here hanging. I have that assurance because of all I walked through. Being on the other side of it, I have no fear. And that is the power of vulnerability. Any time you have a call and you *know* this is something you're supposed to be doing, it requires you to be vulnerable, because vulnerability takes courage. As long as you refuse to allow yourself to feel and to be vulnerable — as in my past choice to refuse to let my husband love me — you are blocking your blessings! We have to choose life; it doesn't just happen. So, I am choosing my life now rather than my life choosing me.

God does not want us to miss our blessings. It was my children who motivated me. I don't want them to miss *their* blessings. I don't want them to work hard. We work at jobs we were never designed to work. The gifts that God put inside us are supposed to create wealth that can be passed on to our kids. Instead, we pass our *issues* on to our kids, who experience even more rejection and abandonment issues than we did. We're not present to parent, because we're too tired … and because of that tiredness, we're angry and frustrated. Next thing we know, our kids have turned to crime, substance abuse or even suicide because of what they have been going through. And all they wanted was us.

The only way we can change this is to get back home to our babies. Back in the day, the old folks were at home, tending to the kids. Where did we drop the ball? They told us to go to work, get a 401k. And then when we work these jobs, we're frustrated and unfulfilled. Again, we're limiting ourselves. And then we're scared, because we have become so dependent on the job that we won't step out there on faith so that we can experience the abundance. We settled for the paycheck because we're scared. (Those at the other end of the spectrum were encouraged to find a way to get a government check. We were never supposed to depend on the government to take care of us.)

Let me tell you something. When you do step out there on faith, there's a frequency that you'll have to vibrate from; when you do, the money will have to show up. When our backs are against the wall, we get creative. We start looking for ways to prosper. That's when we really tap into our power. And then what happens? It manifests, even if it's in that last hour. It's our frequency. Remember me bringing that up in Chapter Two? When our back is up against that wall, our frequency goes up. God says, *Oh, OK, I've got to deliver. Her head and her heart are in alignment. She knows what she needs, and there are no discrepancies in her now. She's got to have this!* Voila! We have become the current that created our currency. But as long as we stay comfortable, nothing happens for us.

In 2020, I believe God wants us to have 2020 vision. He wants us to see clearly. We have only seen one part. This particular year, I believe, is designed for us to see the physical and the spiritual to make the two one again, and for us to possess the land.

It's a new decade. There are supposed to be new opportunities manifesting, new business manifesting … whatever we want. But as long as we only see one 20, and fail to see the other 20, we're going to be limited. *If you believe in you, and who God created you to be, there are no limits except the ones you put on yourself.*

Xhale to Xcel is the subject of not just an empowerment weekend, but also a workshop I developed after being instructed by the Holy Spirit. *Help them identify what they desire, then realize that they're accusing somebody else of not giving it to them,* He said. *The reason they can't identify the problem, and are therefore frustrated about it, is because they haven't given it to themselves; they don't know how. And because society has taught them to look outside themselves for these things, they stay in pursuit of them. Help them [work-shop participants] identify where they're stuck.*

The Spirit instructed me to do seven sessions of this workshop — the number seven being the number of completion. Eight is the number of new beginnings; the eighth session will represent this. During this session, we'll do a destination wedding. It doesn't matter whether a participant is married or single. We have to take the journey to healing ourselves if we're going to heal our marriages and our families.

For more information about this workshop, contact me at www.ChristelWest.com.

ABOUT THE BOOK

$\mathcal{I}$t wasn't enough for me to simply uncover the treasure within. I had to now take the journey to healing all the lies I accepted as truth. I thought I was ready because I finally discovered me. The truth was, I didn't *know* me. I didn't know my likes, dislikes, what made me happy, or even what I enjoyed doing. This new journey required me to love *me* with no conditions and without judgement. I'd judged myself so harshly that, in order to *heal* myself, I had to *forgive* myself. I had to learn to let go. I had to trust that the answers I so longed for — and which seemed to be infinitely hidden from me — would also be found within me.

Thus, *The Journey to My Healing* began with an Xhale. I had to dive headfirst into my past, which housed so much pain, turmoil and chaos, and find the truth of who I was and who I was predestined to be. I had to apply love in the areas of my life that I'd neglected. Taking this walk has allowed me to identify the place where my development was arrested and my growth was halted, giving me the power to break free from my painful past and move forward. I no longer exist in my pain, or my past. I am a free spirit who chooses to live in the now.

If you're ready to Xhale to Xcel … Let Go to Grow … Release, Rise and Reign … Divorce That Story and Marry Your Truth … then this book, and the conferences and workshops I am creating around it, are for you.

Stay tuned. There may be more journeys to come.

BIOGRAPHY

*C*hristel West is a woman born again as her true self. A woman of strength, enlightenment, courage and wisdom. A wife, mother, grandmother, author, success coach and entrepreneur.

Christel's mission is to empower you by promoting your healthy relationship with yourself ... the prerequisite for the journey to becoming your true self.

Christel's mission and purpose were formed through her own personal battles and hardships as a voiceless child, a teenage mother, a victim of molestation and a divorcee. As she was enlightened to rise up and heal herself, she realized this journey was not for her alone. If she could do it, she could assist others in taking the journey back to find their treasure within. This led to the birth of her published memoir *The Journey Back to Me*, the eight-week She Said

Yes course, and her new release, *Xhale to Xcel: The Journey to My Healing*.

Christel's message is clear and precise: YOU MUST DISSOLVE IT IN YOU TO DISSOLVE IT AROUND YOU.

To know more about Christel West, the She Said Yes course and her Xhale to Xcel experiences, or to order a copy of her new release, go to <u>www.ChristelWest.com</u>.

TESTIMONIALS:

XHALE TO XCEL WOMEN'S EMPOWERMENT WEEKEND

I'm the youngest of my siblings – the "baby" — and still living at home. My living status led to the development of a mindset that I wasn't functioning as an adult. Some people told me, "You've got it made!" I didn't feel that way. I lost over 70 pounds, but my self-esteem, my chakra, was still low. Negativity and self-doubt led to feelings of failure and rejection; I felt that I wasn't enough. I didn't know what I wanted, and I certainly didn't know where to start my life's work. I went around asking everyone else for their ideas and suggestions for me as I felt the decisions I had made were not significant. But OOO-WEE! I attended an Xhale to Xcel weekend and learned that I *am* enough. I learned that I could make the right decisions about what I wanted. I learned to love myself first. I learned that I don't have to DO – that just BEING is enough. I learned that I have to have a stable mind when it comes to what I want.

Christel West, I'm FOREVER THANKFUL and GRATE-FUL for you seeing in me the DIAMOND that I am! You are an absolute blessing to me. I see the results in you. I want you to continue to hold me accountable so that I will continue to walk it like I talk it. I LOVE YOU TO LIFE!!

Earlisha Willis, Oklahoma

On Nov. 1, 2019, my outlook on life changed dramatically. As I prepared to go to an Xhale to Xcel event in Little Rock, AR, life threw so many obstacles at me that I thought about giving up and canceling the trip. But the better part of my spirit kept saying, *Don't give up. Keep going.* The pull was so strong that I felt there was something there that I was supposed to get ... something that a part of me was afraid to want, but desired very badly. So, I kept pushing. In my pushing, the better part of me was birthed. I released — and am still releasing — past hurts and shedding all the negative beliefs that I wasn't enough. I have spent my entire 62 years of life proving people wrong when they label me. It took me 53 years to be able to look at myself in a mirror and think I was pretty. At this Xhale to Xcel event, I finally realized that I AM ENOUGH. I realize that all these years, I have been a human doer instead of a human being. Well, NO MORE will I give a damn what others' opinions of me are. That's their business, not mine. NO MORE will I deny myself the love I looked for from outside when it was within me all the time. I'm learning to love my whole self. The best part of what I learned is this: I AM WORTHY and I am ENOUGH!

Tommie O'Neal, Mississippi

When I was 11 years old, I was molested by one of my cousins. They were a year older than I, so I don't think they knew that what they were doing was wrong. I just told my mom that I didn't want to go over to their house anymore. Matter of fact, I never told anyone in my family about the molestation. My baby brother found out about it seven years ago, when I shared my experience with a group of people. Unfortunately, my daughter was also molested at the age of 11. I was married to her stepfather at the time. I was a very hard sleeper, but one particular night, something told me to get up and go check on my child. I walked in on my ex-husband on top of my baby. I told him to leave and called my best friend as well as the police. My ex went to jail. I blamed myself for a long time after this.

When I told my story at the Xhale to Xcel women's empowerment weekend, it affected other women in the room because similar traumas had happened to them.

I just want to thank Christel West for giving women a platform to tell their truth and letting them know this: It's time to stop bringing your representative with you. It's time to unmask and just be you. You may just be helping someone who is going through the exact same thing,

I am a strong woman because of my journey.

Stacie Boyce Page, Mississippi

Not long ago, I was wondering why I was even living. I was feeling lost and sorry for myself … complaining about always loving and doing for so-called family members and friends, only to get my feelings hurt or made to feel like I wasn't enough. I felt those I was showing love didn't love or care for me in return. I would always overlook things, sweep things under the rug, apologize for wrongs I wasn't responsible for — all in hopes of keeping the peace. I eventually felt like I was on the brink of going over the edge. I was tired of all these folks acting as if they cared about me! I was so depressed, I would curl up in a fetal position and lie in bed every chance I got.

I attended an Xhale to Xcel weekend and, welp ... Christel called me out! She told me I was fake. That's why people were fake with me! I wasn't being my true self with them; their actions reflected what I was showing them. I needed to STOP BEING FAKE! Light bulb!!!

I'm so grateful that I went to the event. It renewed my spirit and made me realize IT'S MY TIME to love ME. People will be who they are going to be. But I MUST be who I am, unapologetically. Now I'm on my journey to healing from all the hurt that I've probably inflicted upon myself. I'm not looking back, because I can't change the past! My thanks to Christel and all my fellow Xhale to Xcel attendees for the sisterhood and camaraderie as we came to believe in ourselves and came to know that we all matter and are loved!

Pat Murray Thomas, New York

The Xhale to Xcel event brought out some feelings I had tucked away for years. I got in touch with these feelings — emotional scars from some VERY dark years in my life. I learned that it's OK ... I AM ENOUGH! I saw though the darkness in coming to the realization that everybody has baggage. I thought it was "just me." I learned that it's NOTHING to be ASHAMED of! Until you face YOUR fears, you will carry guilt, shame and indecisiveness

FOREVER! I want to thank all the ladies who attended for sharing their lives with me. Thank you, Christel, for the most exhilarating, incredible, riveting weekend of my life. I have found my "tribe"! I RISE UP!

Felicia Carter Moore, Little Rock, AR

The Xhale to Xcel event was simply amazing. Where do I begin? It was a judgment-free zone where we could truly be ourselves and be vulnerable. I'm an introvert, but I bonded with the other ladies and I allowed myself to be vulnerable. I did karaoke (something I normally don't do!). I told the voice in my head — the one that was concerned about what everybody would think — to shut up. You have to participate in your success, so I did. There was so much information that impacted my life.

You can't expect another person to treat you better than *you* treat you. And you can't expect another person to commit to you at a level higher than you commit to yourself. Love yourself. Commit to yourself. Show up for you and be consistent. Pursue you as if you were pursuing something you can't live without.

Thank you, Christel West. Can't wait until the next event.

Sabrina Black, Little Rock

Xhale to Xcel was so beautiful!! My experience was phenomenal! So much growth! I heard so many stories that related to mine. And seeing these women in their 30/40/50s having the courage to be their true selves ... to actually do the work to genuinely be happy ... gave me confidence to do it for myself! I'm so blessed to call Christel West my mother! Because of her, I have the keys to take on life with the perspective of being my true self. It's truly a beautiful thing!

I look forward to my future, and to more events. Thank you, thank you, thank you, Christel, for being so selfless. You are truly an angel!!

Aleah Weaver, Little Rock

When I was a little girl, I played dress-up with my cousins. We would use towels on our heads for long hair and put on our mothers' robes and get my grandmother's coffee cups and saucers and pretend we were out for a night on the town. We had so much fun, and you couldn't tell us we were not BEAUTIFUL. Because of all the pain and abuse I suffered as I got older, I lost that little girl. I lost my ability to even *dream* of anything good for me ... UNTIL THE XHALE TO XCEL WEEKEND!!!!!! I FOUND HER!!!! I FOUND THAT LITTLE GIRL WHO WAS NEVER AFRAID TO DREAM, BE OR DO ANYTHING!!!! I

AM IN TEARS WRITING THIS ALL OVER AGAIN. Thank you, Christel West, for being obedient to the Holy Spirit. You were my Harriet Tubman, so I had no need to see the 2019 movie *Harriet*. Your obedience reminded me of just who I am. You showed us how Queens should be treated at ALL TIMES. I love you immensely for serving on this awesome level. I AM FREE TO BE AND SO IT IS!

Bridgette Parker Yelder, Atlanta

Coaching Testimonials

I have been on a quest to find what Elsa in *Frozen 2* sang about — "Into the Unknown." Two thousand three, to be exact, is the year I knew I was consciously looking. I have come a long way since then. In 2018, I was told I needed a stern spiritual leader to guide me. Two thousand eighteen kicked my behind on a level that I knew was taking me to a place I would not be able to handle alone. My spiritual journey had begun. I had to pray, surrender and allow God to allow my spirit to be found by the one He'd called to walk me through this season. I put on paper (wrote the vision and made it plain): "I need a spiritual coach!"

When I heard Christel West's voice, it was like that Scripture that says, "My sheep know my voice." Twenty twenty is the year I make my vision clear! Christel's coaching has taken me to a level I didn't know existed. She has taken me "Into the Unknown!"

Laverne Cheeseboro

Christel West is the "bomb dot com." She is amazing! She has shown me the importance of doing that internal work, that soul work! I'm doing my soul work and I can see where I'm going. She is a true blessing in my life. My sistah is amazing. Let her bless your life!!!

Darlaina Rose

As a woman who has experienced many traumas in my life, I became very cold over the years. I was closed and afraid to even think of having anything good in my life … until I began to work on me. While on my personal-development journey, I met Mrs. Christel West. She is a vibrant woman who, by her leadership, has helped me walk boldly into my healing. Her willing spirit when it came to doing her work encouraged me to do my work all the more. She taught me that I am a mirror, and that what I receive is only a reflection of what is inside of me. So, by healing myself, I am able to change what I have been experiencing. I attended the Xhale to Xcel Women's Empowerment event and through Christel's guidance, I opened myself up and found the little girl who was never afraid to dream big. I am using the courage that little girl had to become the Healed Woman who will attract healthy, whole relationships moving forward. I have the tools I can use to direct my life in the way I desire to go, and I thank Christel for helping me find and love *me*.

Bridgette Parker Yelder

Made in the USA
Monee, IL
17 March 2021

63038624R00079